MISDIRECTION FOOTBALL:

Creating the Offensive Edge

MISDIRECTION FOOTBALL:

Creating the Offensive Edge

by

MIKE KOEHLER

Parker Publishing Company, Inc.   **West Nyack, N.Y.**

© 1981 *by*

Parker Publishing Company, Inc.
West Nyack, New York

Library of Congress Cataloging in Publication Data

Koehler, Mike
     Misdirection football.

     Includes index.
     1. Football—Offense.   2. Football coaching.
I. Title.
GV951.8.K63   796.332′2   81-9631
                            AACR2

ISBN 0-13-586099-7

Printed in the United States of America

Dedication

To my daughters Kathleen, Carrie, and Peggy for their love of sports and, particularly, to my wife, Pat, for her warmth and for her love.

Foreword

During the past several years, Deerfield High School has maintained one of the top football programs in the country. They have won their conference championship three times in the last four years and have participated in the state's play-off competition four different times. They won the state championship in 1975, also having achieved the mythical national championship that year. They also were runners-up to the state champs in 1977. In 1980, they were not eliminated until the semi-final game. Having reviewed their films on several different occasions, I am convinced that Deerfield has developed one of the most sophisticated offenses in the nation.

The substance of this book, Deerfield's misdirection offense, represents the single most important component of their offensive attack. It combines deception with power and provides a variety of exciting but fundamentally sound running and passing plays. It has been the mainstay of their attack for several years and gradually has evolved from a simple variation of the old cross buck to a variety of quick openers, traps, counters, and play-action passes. It enables them to hit every hole in a variety of ways and to alter their blocking schemes in order to accommodate almost any kind of defensive adjustment.

Deerfield's misdirection plays are so well-conceived that they can complement any existing offense by adding a new dimension to game strategy. This book is a must for any coach, but particularly for the high school coach who wants to increase the unpredictability of his offense in order to keep his opponents honest and to introduce added excitement for fans on game days.

George Kelly
Assistant Football Coach
The University of Notre Dame

Creating the Offensive Edge with Misdirection Football

Unpredictability is, perhaps, the single most important characteristic of any misdirection offense. Regardless of offensive set, the elements of misdirection explained in this book enable the offense to hit any hole along the line of scrimmage in a variety of ways with a variety of blocking schemes. In addition to providing this element of unpredictability, a complement of misdirection plays can help your program in several specific ways.

The diversity of plays enables the offense to break its own tendencies by formation, hence to counteract defensive adjustments which the opponent derives from scouting reports. The process of scouting yourself (Chapter 10), a very simple and routine responsibility for one of your game statisticians, identifies your own tendencies by down and formation and enables you to break those tendencies by using the same formations but by using misdirection plays to vary the offensive attack.

Misdirection, because it is incorporated into your existing offense, is easily learned by your players and provides the diversity needed to transform routine timing drills into purposeful practice sessions. Players will feel more invested in the offense and practice more conscientiously when they realize its sophistication and strategic effectiveness.

Misdirection enables the offense to attack the weak side of an overshifted defense. Once defensive stunts and adjustments have been identified by the offense, misdirection enables the offense to attack weaknesses without changing offensive formations or altering the game plan.

Misdirection can attack and defeat 5-2 defenses at their strongest point, the "bubble." If the offense is run correctly, a stunting noseman will never guess right. More importantly, misdirection plays confuse the keys of linebackers and the defensive secondary, especially in situations involving the tackle trap. Inside linebackers in the 5-2 are immobilized by backfield action and are unable to read through the offensive guard to determine trap action.

The effectiveness of play-action passes is increased because of the inability of the defensive secondary to maintain their keys and to anticipate anything other than misdirection when the offensive backs execute their fakes well. They can transform a normally tough, well-adjusted safety into a red-faced, fire-breathing madman. A streamlined way of calling pass plays and of coordinating them with misdirection is explained in Chapter 8 and will be very helpful to coaches.

Coaches who may be having problems simplifying their method of calling formations in the huddle or in scouting reports will find our formation-calling system in Chapter 1 to be very helpful. It has given us the flexibility to run our offense from hundreds of formations and to challenge the sanity of the opposing coach who scouts us and has to determine our tendencies by formation.

A well executed misdirection offense assists offensive linemen with their blocking responsibilities by keeping defensive personnel honest and by creating excellent blocking angles, especially on misdirection plays involving the tackle trap.

Chapter 9 outlines the strategic advantages of combining motion with misdirection. Aside from the simple advantage of creating a numerical imbalance toward either end of the line of scrimmage, motion causes the unprepared team to question its keys and to doubt its planned defense for the game. And once the defense adjusts to the motion, misdirection enables the offense to counteract the adjustments. The defense can't win.

Practicing misdirection must be ongoing throughout the year because it requires so much precision. Chapter 11 discusses key elements in effective practice sessions from the first few days up to the last few weeks of the season. A sample practice schedule is provided to give evidence of our emphasis on fundamentals as well as on the frequent repetition of our backfield execution.

The chapter on strategy will enable coaches to "outsmart" rather than to "overpower" their opponents. Standard defensive keys, such as safety keys on the home halfbacks and middle linebacker keys on the fullback, although effective much of the time, will lead defensive players *away* from misdirection plays. Such keys will work to the offense's advantage. The more quickly the defenders read their keys and get into their pursuit paths, the more successful misdirection will be. After having used several misdirection plays, offenses will be better able to overpower teams because defenses no longer will be able to rely on keys to gang up on them. Again, misdirection action capitalizes on that key word "unpredictability" and will complement, not replace, your basic offense.

This complementary relationship also will be discussed as it applies to the offenses of a few major universities. The continued dominance of Michigan, Nebraska, and Oklahoma make them perfect examples of successful misdirection strategies. The head coach of each school responded to a questionnaire which surveyed his school's use of misdirection. The results are in Chapter 12.

Some of their misdirection plays and all of Deerfield High School's misdirection plays are described in this book. Each is diagrammed versus basic defenses, and each is described in terms of basic backfield alignments and their

variations. The book provides an excellent resource to the
football coach who is seeking greater diversity in his offensive attack.

Misdirection plays can transform a collection of basic
series into a sophisticated and unpredictable offensive attack. Their introduction into your offense will not require a
complete overhauling or, for that matter, discarding of your
playbook. All that will be required is that you add several
pages. Those several pages, however, will provide a whole
new dimension to your offense and will introduce the strategic concepts you require to develop and maintain a championship football program.

Mike Koehler

Acknowledgments

I would like to thank Freddie Harris for the tackle trap, Ron O'Connor for his pass plays, George Kelly for his connections, Paul Adams for organizing such a potent offense, and Greg Royer for bouncing ideas around. They have no idea how helpful they were.

I also would like to thank Coaches Switzer, Osborne, and Schembechler for their help with the last chapter. Their contributions to football already are legendary.

And, again, I would like to thank my wife, Pat, for the typing and the reading ... as well as for her support and patience.

Contents

MISDIRECTION FOOTBALL:

Creating the Offensive Edge

1

The How-to Basics
of a Good Misdirection
Offense

No addition to a playbook of basic offense series will provide the strategic effectiveness and the excitement of a complement of misdirection plays. The sophistication and the diversity they provide transform a basic, conventional offense into a surprisingly unpredictable ground and air attack. Misdirection will revitalize your program for players and fans alike. Your teams will have fun running these plays. Nothing peps up a practice like the introduction and the execution of several plays that the players absolutely believe in. Your fans will have fun watching them. You will have fun calling them. And your opponents will be unable to determine with any consistency where you intend to run the ball. No longer will they be able to stack defenses against you. Tendencies by formation, down and distance, even field position no longer will serve them as indicators of your offensive game plan. The addition of misdirection will enhance your unpredictability and will become a dependable, consistently effective, and exciting part of your game strategy.

Misdirection Terminology

Although the terminology in this book is familiar to most coaches, several of the terms require a definition in order that we can speak a common language throughout the book.

The first term probably is familiar to you. It is the focal point of the book, however, so it is the first to be defined.

1. Misdirection

Misdirection involves one player, usually the ball carrier, moving against backfield flow. It normally hits the point of attack more slowly than plays from basic series and may involve multiple handoffs, although it usually involves only one. Misdirection can happen in a variety of ways: slant traps, counter plays, crossbucks, reverses, bootlegs, ends around, or crossfire action (this latter term will be the focus of Chapter 3). Normally, it does not constitute a series in and of itself but represents variations within one or more basic series.

2. Flexed End

Contrasted with the split end, who may be positioned up to twenty yards outside the offensive tackle, the flexed end is positioned only five to six yards from the tackle, up to a maximum of eight yards.

3. Down Blocking

Down blocking refers to the angle block created when one or more offensive linemen are assigned the man on their inside shoulder. An effective down block may be executed with a near head and shoulder or with a reverse head and shoulder block, the block to be determined by the skills and techniques of the defensive player and by the needs of the play to be run. These blocks are discussed later in the book.

4. Counter Action

Counter action is backfield movement that looks like a counter play. It is used to camouflage a basic play. If the formation, for example, is a Pro set with a Wingback and if the play call involves the fullback in a straight dive play, "counter action" will involve the wingback in a fake after the ball has been handed off to the fullback. Such backfield action is especially effective if several misdirection plays already have been run and if the defense, especially the safeties and the defensive halfbacks, are keying the wingback and are anticipating the counter play. This concept and its strategy are discussed at length in Chapter 10.

5. Flat Motion

Constrasted with regular motion, wherein the motion man may be as far from the line of scrimmage as the deepest man in the backfield, flat motion places a wingback, slot-back, or flankerback in motion only three to five feet off the line of scrimmage and parallel to it. Flat motion may be executed into or away from the sideline, depending upon the strategic needs of the play.

6. Double Digit Plays

Double digit plays such as the 12 and 21 traps start the ball carrier toward one hole then veer him toward another. The 12 trap requires the fullback to take his initial step toward the one hole, in our case toward the offensive left guard, then veer to the two hole, toward the offensive right guard. The opposite would be true of the 21 trap.

Double digit plays provide a different dimension to misdirection and are presented at length in Chapter 4. One such play, however, the Crossfire 12 trap, is illustrated in Chapter 2.

7. Finesse Blocking

Finesse blocking is more a scheme of blocking than a method of execution. The defensive man to be "finessed," generally on the line of scrimmage, simply is not blocked. Such a blocking scheme is used strategically by many offenses, but most notably by proponents of the Houston Veer and the triple option.

8. "On" and "Off"

"On" is a term used to designate the side of the line of scrimmage which involves the point of attack. The left guard, therefore, would be the "on guard" if the play were being run behind the left tackle and the left guard. In such a circumstance, the right end's assignment would be to block downfield "on." Conversely, the term "off" is used to designate the side of the line of scrimmage which is away from the point of attack. Were the play run behind the left tackle, the right guard would be designated "guard off."

A Better Way to Call Formations

"Keep it simple" is a guiding principle for every experienced football coach. Simplicity is the essence not only of creativity but also of a well-conceived formation and play-calling system. Players have enough to do on the field; they do not need the added pressure of decoding the verbal hieroglyphics of a poorly designed method of calling formations. Several years ago, we developed a concise, yet sophisticated method of getting players in the right places at the right times. It has simplified our process so dramatically that we have increased the sophistication of using multiple sets while avoiding unnecessary confusion for our players. The method, in and of itself, may be helpful to you in simplifying or in replacing your system for calling formations. It involves a minimum of words and provides clear direction for every player. It also facilitates scouting your opponents as well as yourself, a procedure which will be discussed at length in Chapter 8. A primary reason for its inclusion in this chapter, however, is to help you understand the terminology used in this book. An equally important reason, however, is to give you an important bonus which will help streamline your whole system.

Hole Numbering

Our hole numbering system is not unlike the number systems used by most football teams. Odd numbers designate holes on the left side of the offensive line, even numbers the right side of the line. The *players* are designated numerically, not the splits separating them. The center is numbered zero, the left guard one, the right guard two, and so on. The nine and the ten areas would represent a normal split end or flankerback position, from ten to fifteen yards outside the nearest man on the offensive line.

The numbering system, therefore, because it represents a position on the offensive line, can be used to designate the point of attack as well as to describe the offensive formation. All running backs are encouraged on every play to note the positioning of the player representing the point of attack. The offensive right tackle, for example, on a play run at the four hole may want an additional one to two foot split to gain a blocking angle. The running back has to notice the tackle's adjusted position in order to hit the right hole. Numbering players instead of areas between players on the offensive line provides the flexibility to allow the hole "to move" a few feet, if need be.

How to Call Your Formations

Such a numbering system allows us to simplify our procedure for calling offensive formations. We use five basic backfield alignments: the "I" (with variations), the "T," the Fullhouse, the Wing, and the Pro formations. Each is illustrated in Figures 1-1 through 1-5.

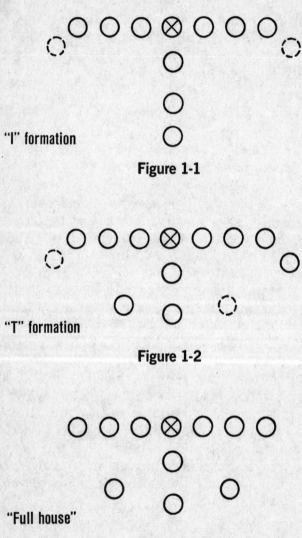

"I" formation

Figure 1-1

"T" formation

Figure 1-2

"Full house"

Figure 1-3

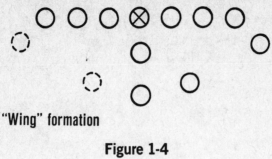

"Wing" formation

Figure 1-4

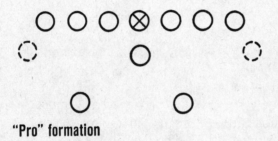

"Pro" formation

Figure 1-5

Our method of calling formations involves a left to right description along the offensive line. Only players whose normal "home" positions are to be adjusted are affected by the formation call. If, for example, no position adjustments are required, no formation call will be made in the huddle, and the team will line up with two tight ends and a "fullhouse" backfield. If variations are required, however, the formation call would begin with the left end, would be followed by the backfield set, and would conclude with the right end. The formation illustrated in Figure 1-6, therefore, would be called "Open-Pro 6-Split." The term "open" is used to designate the positioning of the *left* end; "split" designates the *right* end. Such terminology avoids the unnecessary confusion in the huddle that might follow a *"Split*-Pro 6-

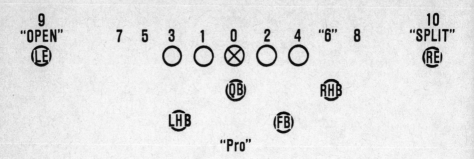

"Open-Pro 6-Split"

Figure 1-6

Split" designation, assuming that both ends are to be adjusted. Anything we can do to keep it simple is going to pay big dividends in the long run.

If the left end were to be flexed as opposed to split, that is, positioned only five to six yards away from the left tackle, the call would be "Flex-Pro 6-Split."

If neither end were to be affected by the formation called, and the backfield set were a pro with a wingback, the call would be either "Pro 8" or "Pro 7." Refer to Figure 1-7.

If the backfield set were a pro with a flanker, it would be "Pro 10" or "Pro 9." See Figure 1-8.

If only the left end were split and the backfield set were a wing with a flanker, the call would be "Open-Wing 10." See Figure 1-9.

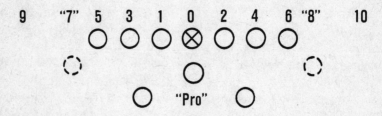

"Pro 8" or "Pro 7"

Figure 1-7

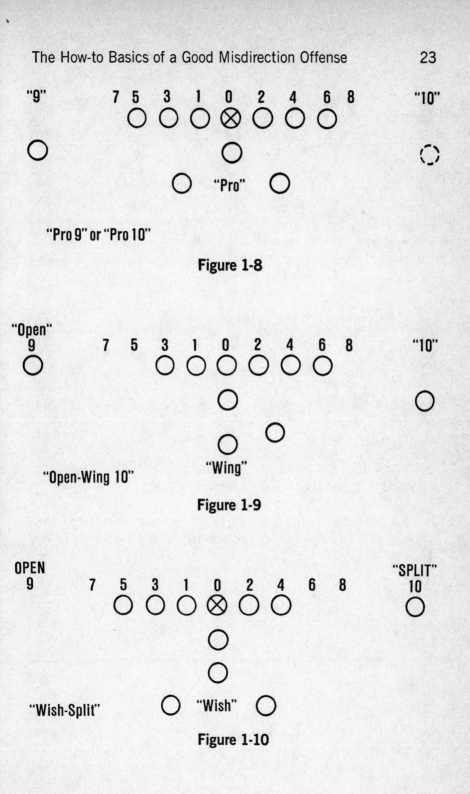

"9"   7 5   3   1   0   2   4   6   8   "10"

"Pro"

"Pro 9" or "Pro 10"

Figure 1-8

"Open" 9   7   5   3   1   0   2   4   6   8   "10"

"Open-Wing 10"   "Wing"

Figure 1-9

OPEN 9   7   5   3   1   0   2   4   6   8   "SPLIT" 10

"Wish-Split"   "Wish"

Figure 1-10

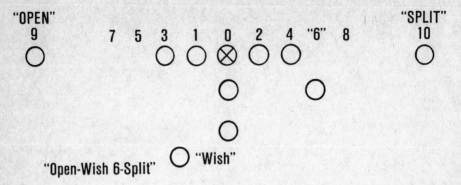

"Open-Wish 6-Split"

Figure 1-11

The variations are endless—and all very easy to call. Imagine in your own mind what each of the following would look like: "Wing 9," "I 6-Split," "Open T 8," and "Flex-Pro 8."

Consider the Wishbone. Whether scouting another team or designating one of our own formations, we can easily describe the Wishbone and its variations. Figure 1-10 illustrates a "Wish-Split." Figure 1-11 illustrates a fancier call: "Open-Wish 6-Split."

Additional Misdirection Formations

In addition to these formations, we have run out of the Spread, the Shotgun, and the Double Wing formations. We have chosen in the past to designate the Double Wing as such in the huddle or, when concerned with consistency, have called it an "I 78." Each designation has been acceptable to our players. They generally have mastered our formation-calling system by the end of the first couple days of practice. From then on we feel free to introduce variations, such as the "I 78" designation, which is not a normal call for us.

A myriad of additional variations is possible. Consider the "Pro 4" or even the "Pro 2" formations as ways to gang up on the middle of a 5-2 defense. However, we will call such formations only occasionally; they are not suited to the basic offense.

The purpose in this section was to familiarize you with our formation designation system, perhaps as a tool for you to use in simplifying or in replacing your system, and also to enable us to use a common language throughout the remainder of the book.

With that thought in mind, the next consideration involves "who" is needed to run a good misdirection offense.

What to Look For in Personnel

Complementing your basic series with a host of misdirection plays will not require the services of uniquely gifted athletes. If football teams enjoyed the services, year after year, of uniquely gifted athletes, schools would not need coaches to plan strategy. All coaches would have to do is teach the players a little blocking and tackling, throw in a few plays, and then get out of the way. Unfortunately, or fortunately as the case may be, most football teams, high school teams in particular, work each year (if they're lucky) with only a few stand-out ball players, the rest of the team composed of willing and dedicated but generally limited players. The coach's job, then, is to use that personnel efficiently and to devise game strategy which capitalizes not only on player strengths but on opponent weaknesses.

To run misdirection effectively, therefore, only a few positions are critical. That the tackle position is one of the most critical is no surprise to anyone. Tackles are critical within any play. Their positioning on any onside action places them right in the middle of the action. The misdirection offense requires that they be not only big and tough but also mobile. Because all the counter plays to be described in Chapter 4 involve the tackle trap, tackles must be quick enough to lead the wingback to the hole and mobile enough to execute the trap block once they get there.

Some teams execute misdirection with guard traps but, by doing so, continue to provide a key to middle linebackers or to inside linebackers in the 5-2 who read *through* the guards to their backfield keys. Tackle traps eliminate that key and momentarily may confuse defensive safeties who misinterpret the tackle's move as a down block or an on-side seal, thereby making misdirection even more effective.

Another key position is the wingback, who must have the quickness to get to the hole and the kinesthetic sense to make the right moves once he gets there. Because the defense generally will be immobilized if the play is run effectively, the ball carrier rarely will be expected to cut back against the grain. He may be expected, however, to juke a safety or to make a lateral outside move on the defensive halfback. Such moves require quickness and good speed.

The wingback also must possess good pass-receiving abilities. Generally the wingback will be on the wing position; occasionally he may be slotted or, more often, flankered. At such times and depending upon the strategic needs of the team, good pass-receiving skills will be essential. During play action passes he will have to be smart enough to "stalk" the defensive halfback or the safety in order to simulate an intended block, quick enough to make the transition into his pass route, and skilled enough to catch the ball.

Depending upon a team's personnel situation and the needs of its basic offensive series, both halfbacks may be used as wingbacks. If a team, however, has but one running back with the quickness and the pass-receiving capability to play the position, he may be designated the wingback on every play, regardless of the backfield set. The other backs, who may be quick but not skilled enough at pass receiving, may be designated the running backs. Neither situation is preferrable over the other. Each can be effective but is dependent upon the special talents of the team's personnel.

Two additional personnel needs are important but are not critical. Because the fullback is focal within just about every play, he must be able to read the hole, a particularly important talent, especially on crossfire action. Strong, fast backs with no reading ability will help the team somewhere but not at fullback, especially in the misdirection/crossfire offense. Crossfire traps and other misdirection plays require the talents of fullbacks who "run to daylight," even if they may not be quite as big or as fast as some of the other backs on the team. But they must be big enough to break an arm tackle and to fill for the offensive tackle on misdirection counter plays.

The other personnel need involves the offensive guards, who must be big enough to conceal backfield action and to area block, especially against stunting nosemen and blitzing linebackers. Because each of these personnel needs generally is true of every other offense, they are not restricted to the misdirection offense. But they help.

The skill requirements of the other positions are the same as those needed within basic series. For that reason, they need not be mentioned. What is important, however, is to put people in the right spots with a minimum of confusion and to use them wisely.

Let's Wrap It Up

Misdirection, if added hastily to a basic offense, can succeed only in confusing your players. It is more sophisticated than most series and requires simple and clear communication. I recall years ago my old high school coach assaulting us with the saying that the day of the dumb football player is over. I guess I believed at the time that some football players may have been dumb. I have discovered since then that some still are. I have also discovered that coaches are not; some are just shortsighted. And any combination of dumb football players and shortsighted coaches loses football games.

But most players, just about all of them in fact, will learn anything we teach them, if we avoid unnecessary confusion. Once terminology or concepts get needlessly complicated, players are no longer able to concentrate on the tasks at hand. When that happens, the team loses.

So remember to keep it simple. The formation-calling

system which was introduced in this chapter is easily adaptable to any offense and will communicate clearly to any player. It will also do wonders for your scouting format. The system will simplify terminology for your players, and it will make your job a lot easier

2

The When of
Misdirection

It's Time to Talk Strategy

The case *for* the misdirection offense has been made.
Many teams need the unpredictability it provides. *When* to
use it becomes the next important question. Even the best
conceived offenses lose games if coaches fail to sequence
properly and to identify weaknesses in the defense. Misdirection, like every other part of the offensive game, is effective
only if it is called at the right time. Random guessing and
hoping might work once in a while but, more often than not,
coaches who guess run out of luck sooner than their opponents. A card-playing pal of mine used to say that he would
rather be lucky than smart. I often felt that he never would
have become a very good football coach. Come to think of it,
he wasn't even a very good card player.

What are needed, then, are some consistently reliable
guidelines to govern a coach's use of misdirection. The
following six principles, therefore, presented in order of
importance, will provide the framework for determining the
use of misdirection.

Outsmart Stunting Linebackers

Misdirection can be particularly effective against stunting linebackers, particularly versus the 5-2. Defenses that "deal" with the inside backers and noseman are particularly vulnerable to misdirection. If the center and guards can seal the onside of the line by area blocking a stunting defense, off-tackle counter plays will put pressure on defensive ends and cornerbackers. The strategy is quite simple. The linebackers, having neutralized themselves, are unable to pursue to the outside. The safeties generally are neutralized by backfield action, especially if their backfield keys execute good fakes. The outside man on the defensive line and the defensive halfback are on their own, the defensive end to handle a trapping tackle, the defensive halfback to ward off a block from the offensive tackle and to stop one of the offense's most maneuverable ball carriers. Figure 2-1 presents the defense's predicament. The dotted lines represent standard defensive keys; the action illustrates the strategic effectiveness of misdirection against blitzing linebackers.

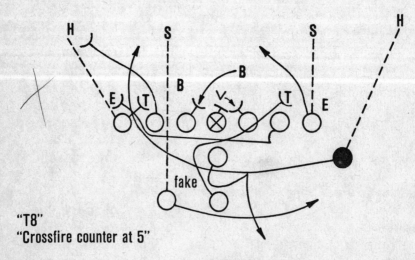

"T8"
"Crossfire counter at 5"

Figure 2-1

As evidenced in the diagram, misdirection transforms a normally effective defensive key into an offensive advantage.

The safety's key on the "home" halfback, for example, probably will remove him completely from the point of attack.
He'll be running one way while the ball carrier is running
the other.

Breaking Mirrors

Misdirection also is effective when the defensive secondary rotates on action, that is, when they *mirror* the
movement of the offensive backfield. Such defensive rotation
is inevitable if the defensive halfbacks or cornerbackers are
keying the offensive ends and if the safeties in a four deep
defense are keying the home halfbacks. Because these keys
are standard within most defenses, misdirection is particularly effective. If, on the other hand, the defense adjusts
its keys to counteract misdirection, the offense will be able to
run its basic series with greater success, especially if it
occasionally runs the basic plays with "counter action."

Refer to Figure 2-2, which illustrates a routine power
sweep. Note also the defensive secondary rotation, which
results from standard keys, represented by the dotted lines.
The formation is a "Pro 8."

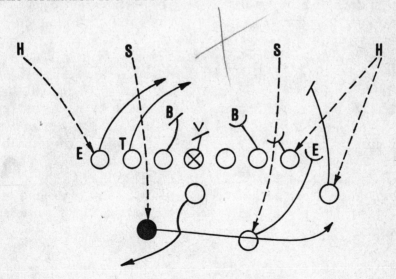

Figure 2-2

Such backfield action is predictable. The success of the power sweep is dependent not only on when it is called but on the strength and the skills of the offensive personnel. The Green Bay Packers during the Lombardi era were a perfect example. "Papa" Vince let the whole world know where he intended to run the ball and then ran it there—successfully—over and over and over. He had the people to do it, and he instilled in them a gut-level belief in themselves and in their teammates. As every coach knows, that kind of belief makes champions of even mediocre football players, and every coach will continue to strive for it in all his players. Not many of us, however, have Jerry Kramers and Jimmy Taylors. The old Green Bay power sweep led each man in the secondary to the point of attack. High schools need a strategic advantage.

On that basis, consider Figure 2-3, a counter play run from the same formation and involving the same keys and the same backfield action. The backfield action leads the defensive secondary, especially the safeties, *away* from the point of attack. In addition, the tackle trap is a much less obvious key for linebackers. If the linebackers are keying through the guards to the "home" backs, they have no clue that the play invovles either a trap or misdirection. This is an important point. When we first conceived of running counters with Tackle Traps, we thought that the strategy was good but that we probably would be unable to find tackles with that kind of mobility. Our worries were short-lived. Every tackle we have had within the past seven years has become an excellent trapper. And the strategy has succeeded in freezing the inside and middle linebackers. Not one of their keys gives them *any* idea of where we are running the ball.

Finally, if the defensive secondary pre-rotates into the wingback, the effectiveness of misdirection is even more evident. One obvious way to coax a defense into a pre-rotated secondary is to run the fullback power from a Wing 8 position. They still may not pre-rotate, but the imbalance between offense and defense will make them think twice, especially if the fullback power is successful.

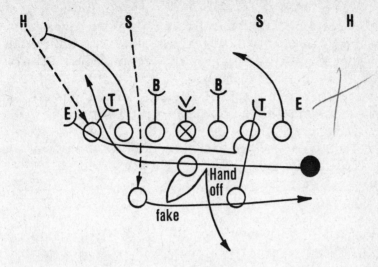

Figure 2-3

In such a circumstance, the counter play is even more effective. And if the defense fails to adjust because it fears the potential for misdirection, the fullback power and anything involving a quarterback rollout would be especially effective. Misdirection places the defense in a "no win" situation.

Beat the Middle Linebacker

Once an offensive team establishes a successful series such as the Crossfire series or the Inside and Outside Belly series, the fullback begins to draw considerable attention from a number of different people on the defensive team. The person who becomes *most* interested in his activities is the middle linebacker. Most middle linebackers will key the fullback, especially if the fullback is in his "home" position; generally, they also will be expected to mirror his movements, because in *most* instances, the fullback will lead the middle linebacker to the point of attack. Not so with the misdirection offense.

Although the middle linebacker's key on the fullback will be reliable when the offense runs its basic series, such a

key will become not only unreliable but an offensive advantage when the offense runs misdirection. An impressive
example of such misdirection is the crossfire 12 or 21 trap.
Although counter plays and slant traps can be equally
effective, the 12 and 21 traps are examples of quick-hitting
misdirection and are particularly effective against well-
skilled and aggressive middle linebackers. More will be said
about the 12 trap in Chapter 4, especially about its strategy
and execution. For now, however, look at Figure 2-4.

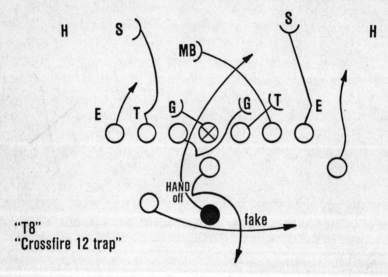

"T8"
"Crossfire 12 trap"

Figure 2-4

Keying the fullback, the middle linebacker's first steps
will be to his right and toward the offensive center, especially
if he's keying through the center's block. That is exactly
where the offense wants him. His reactions, prompted by the
fullback's initial steps, place him in perfect position for the
right tackle's block. Several techniques are available to the
right tackle to get to the middle linebacker, all of which are
in Chapter 4.

Counter plays and slant traps also are effective strategies to use against a good middle linebacker. Each of these strategies is discussed at length in later chapters.

Embarrass the Best of 'Em

The more well-coached the opposing team, the more effective is misdirection. The first few principles governing the use of misdirection capitalize on the standard keys used by most defenses. Misdirection also capitalizes on the occasional mental lapses made by defensive ends and the defensive secondary. When backfield action goes away, for example, most defensive ends are instructed to check for the bootleg, counter, reverse, and screen before pursuing the play downfield. Occasionally, however, and sometimes all too frequently for the defensive coach, the ends and the defensive halfbacks will pursue on backfield action and will forget their follow-up responsibilities. At such times, use misdirection.

A well-coordinated coaching staff on the sidelines, looking for defensive lapses and identifying defensive keys, is essential if the offensive team is to use misdirection at the right time. If assistant coaches know the offensive play call before the play is run and are able to observe the behaviors of specific defensive players during the play, their contributions to necessary offensive adjustments will be increased.

If, for example, the offensive team has been successful running the Inside Belly at 3 or 5, and one of the assistants has determined that the left defensive end is pursuing immediately in order to help out on the other side of the line, an "Inside Belly Counter at 6" would be an excellent call. Consider Figure 2-5.

If the onside defensive halfback is moving on backfield action, too, the play is a likely touchdown. The added advantage of such a misdirection play is that the next time the Inside Belly is run at 3, the linebackers will be less anxious to hurry to the other side of the line.

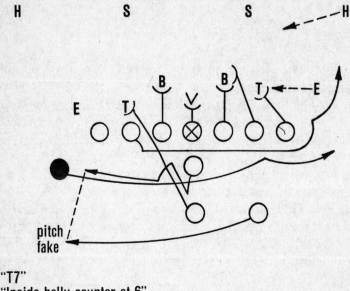

"T7"
"Inside belly counter at 6"

Figure 2-5

Use a Little Finesse

Misdirection also is effective when defensive ends are "boxing," that is penetrating two to three feet and facing up with the backfield action, and when other defensive linemen are penetrating more than a yard beyond the line of scrimmage. In such instances, they are particularly susceptible to counter plays and slant traps. Such defensive maneuvers, however, assist the offensive personnel with the execution of their assignments more than they serve as indications of the need for misdirection. They generally are secondary reasons. The primary reasons to use misdirection involve the defensive keys and the aggressiveness of the defensive players in using them. A boxing defensive end may be so aggressive that the best strategy is to "finesse" him. Don't block him.

Just have the pulling tackle shield him on his way into the
secondary. All the wingback has to do is stay close behind
the tackle and let him do all the work. That's what tackles
get paid for.

If You Don't Need It, Do It Anyway

A final reason to use misdirection capitalizes on its
unpredictability. Use it when you don't need it. Such a
strategy will serve a two-fold purpose. One, it will keep the
defense honest. The opposing team will lose confidence in its
keys and may play more hesitatingly once they have realized
the unpredictability of the offense. When a defense has a
team well-scouted and feels confident that it can predict
plays based on tendency or formation, the offense is in
trouble. It is forced to make sideline or halftime adjustments
in strategy and, generally, if unaware of its own tendencies,
never seems able to overcome the advantages of a well-
prepared defense. The process of scouting yourself to determine your own tendencies, described in a later chapter, and
the use of misdirection to confuse defensive keys serves to
keep defenses guessing. And once the offense has the defense
guessing, the offense generally is at least one step ahead
throughout the entire game.

A second reason to use misdirection when you don't
need it involves the teams that may be scouting your game.
You may be in complete control of the contest and may not
want to show anything other than your most basic series. On
the other hand, even though you may have the game in hand,
you may want the coaches who are scouting you to realize
your potential for misdirection, just as you may want them
to see the same basic plays from as many different backfield
sets as possible. The more they write down, the more they
have to analyze and incorporate into their preparation for
your game. Time is at a premium when preparing to play a
good football team. The more of your opponent's time you tie
up, the less time he has to devote to his own offense. And one
of the great advantages of misdirection is that he will never
be sure when you plan to use it. So use misdirection, even

when you don't need it. You may not gain big yardage at the time, but the threat it provides will help maintain that edge in strategy that you require.

Let's Wrap It Up

"You can't fool a dummy" has been a football truism for years. The intent of the statement is not to insult the intelligence of football players. Rather it recognizes the fact that some teams are better coached than others. Some defenses are instructed to "go out there and play football" with little preliminary coaching regarding defensive keys and pursuit paths. Such teams will not be fooled by misdirection. Generally, they will be fooled by everything else, so misdirection is wasted on them.

Interestingly, the *well-coached* teams are the ones most likely to be embarrassed by misdirection. Well-coached defenses rely heavily on keys and generally are composed of alert, aggressive football players who can stifle a predictable offensive attack. Misdirection provides the tool to transform their aggressiveness and confidence into uncertainty and their use of keys into an offensive advantage.

What is required, however, is that the offensive team does its homework. Review of films, analysis of scouting reports, and a week of hard preparation before each game may not be enough. The old story that good football teams win their games during halftime is still true. Adjustments must be made while the game is in progress. The defense must be analyzed; keys must be determined. All this requires a systematic and well-coordinated sideline approach (to be discussed in Chapter 8). Once this is accomplished, misdirection will become invaluable. It will provide the diversity you need to make those game-winning adjustments.

3

The Crossfire Series:
The Heart of a Good
Misdirection Offense

What Is Crossfire Action?

Remember the old crossbuck? Some of the younger coaches may not, but those of us who suffered the ravages of the Single Wing, with its power sweeps and buck laterals, remember it only too clearly. Ideas never really die, especially good ones. They just lie around a while and eventually appear under a different name. Crossfire action is one such idea. The crossfire series uses the same basic principle of the crossbuck, two or more backs moving in opposite directions. Crossfire action has other characteristics, but the element of misdirection seems to be its most distinctive.

As is the case with other series, crossfire action with us went through several years of evolution, benefitting each year from the sometimes dramatic, sometimes subtle variations introduced by new assistant coaches or by the changing demands being made of our offense. The growing sophistication of defenses introduced variations that capitalized on keys, pursuit paths, and a variety of stunts.

Because of these changes, we found that "straight up stuff" was not working for us. Quick openers and power sweeps were becoming too predictable, and most of our opponents knew where we planned to run the ball, based upon several very obvious tendencies we had developed. Down and distance, even field position became excellent predictors for our opponents. Our most obvious tendency, however, was formation. We got tied in to a complement of basic plays which we ran from certain formations, and we failed to realize that we had become so obvious. To varying degrees, all of us are guilty of this very thing, gradually falling into a very predictable pattern of formation and play calling. Learning how to scout yourself can be one remedy. Misdirection is another.

The crossfire series resulted. It enables us to hit every hole along the line of scrimmage in a variety of ways. With each passing season and with the input of several excellent coaches, the crossfire series evolved from a simple variation of the crossbuck to a variety of traps, counters, and play action passes. This chapter will introduce the basics of the crossfire series. Subsequent chapters will introduce and explain its many variations.

The player most focal within the series is the fullback, because when he is not running the ball he has to immobilize the middle linebacker, and when he is running the ball he has to break one or more arm tackles and read a hole that opens and closes very quickly. The series is most effective when the fullback is in his normal "home" position because crossfire action is designed to hit the point of attack quickly. Most often, when the fullback is running the ball, he either is power running behind the guard's block or is reading the center's block on the nose guard. If the fullback is run from a Pro set into the 0, 1, or 2 holes, generally he will be too late getting there, and the hole will open and close before he gets to the line of scrimmage. So we keep him "at home" directly behind the quarterback when we run Crossfire action. At times we even cheat him up one or two steps, simulating a Wishbone set, especially if the opposing team uses a 5-2 and has a stunting nose guard. Even when the fullback does not run the ball, he at times will cheat up and hit the hole just as quickly, losing himself in the middle of the line by running into the nearest defensive man. Many variations are possible. Undoubtedly, you will develop many of your own, based upon the strategic as well as the personnel needs of your offense.

Once the defensive team starts to ignore the fullback's fake, we can use several crossfire action passes that capitalize on the fullback's pass-catching abilities. We have been running the crossfire series for at least fifteen years and have yet to see a defense that can cover the fullback on pass action. If the backfield action is good and the fullback allows himself to get lost for a count or two in the middle of the line, he invariably will be able to find an open area somewhere in the secondary. Such plays are discussed extensively in Chapter 6.

The crossfire series, then, consists of straight action, play-action passes, inside and off-tackle traps, option plays, counter plays, and screens. It probably is the staple of our offense and does provide a good framework for any team interested in using misdirection. Again, it is not dramatic, nor will it win any awards for creativity, but, as a basic series, it provides everything we need to confuse the defense and to build a solid foundation for the use of misdirection. Above all, it wins football games.

A Few More Plugs for Misdirection

We can hit any hole we want with the crossfire series. One of the best principles underlying the use of misdirection is that it allows the offense to attack any point on the line of scrimmage *from the same backfield set*. This one principle suggests three important advantages. One, it capitalizes on the running abilities of every back and uses each as a running threat, regardless of his positioning in the formation. Two, it suggests the need to slot or wing the third back in order to maintain his threat as a runner as well as a pass receiver. Flanking the third back, especially on obvious pass situations, helps spread the defensive secondary and, in effect, makes the defensive "zones" larger and more difficult to cover. But flanker backs, unless put in motion, do not pose a threat as ball carriers. Even in motion, they rarely pose threats as ball carriers. They do these other things, but they do not put the defense in a "run or pass" dilemma. As wingbacks, especially on first downs, they increase the anxiety levels of the defensive secondary, particularly if the opponent has gained a healthy respect for the offense's potential for misdirection. Three, it discourages defensive teams from "ganging up" on the *obvious* strengths of the offensive set. Effective counter plays and other misdirection strategies suggest threats in addition to the obvious strength of the formation. Most are more subtle and potentially more dangerous, especially if the defense is caught napping. So defenses tend to remain pretty honest.

Crossfire and the "T"

The "T" formation, see Figure 3-1, was determined arbitrarily. It has no special significance other than as a way for us to call this formation with an economy of words. Figure 3-1 illustrates the "T" with a wingback, designated "T 8" in our terminology. Remember that the same formation with a split left end would be designated "Open-T 8." If the right halfback were flankered instead of winged, the formation call would be "T 10". With a split left end, it would be "Open-T 10". Try to master this formation-calling system.

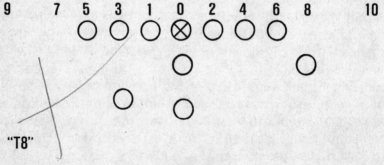

Figure 3-1

Our communication between sideline and huddle no longer requires a runner with a photographic memory, and our scouting system is greatly refined. It will do the same things for you.

Basic Plays

From the "T 8" formation, we can hit every hole along the line of scrimmage. Obviously, some of the plays take a little longer than others to develop, but the weaknesses in the defense may require just that. Most of the longer developing plays, counters and bootlegs, will be discussed in subsequent chapters. For now, we will discuss the quick-hitting plays, the "basics" of the crossfire series.

Crossfires at One and Two, Three and Four, Five and Six

These are the most fundamental plays within the series. The "T 8" formation enables us to run the Crossfires at one (with the fullback) and at four (with the left halfback). To run at two or at three, the backfield set would have to be a "T 7" or a "T 9" or a "T 9—Split" or any of several offensive alignments. Suffice it to say that the halfback must be lined up on the side of the formation away from the point of attack. He must be the left halfback when the play is run at four, the right halfback when it is run at three. When the play is at one (Huddle call: "T 8" "Crossfire at 1"), the quarterback opens into the fullback, hands him the ball, and hand fakes the left halfback, who is running diagonally into the four hole. After executing the handoff and the fake, the quarterback bootleg fakes "on side," that is to the side away from the halfback's fake and *to* the side of the point of attack. See Figure 3-2.

Technique is very important. To conceal the ball most effectively and to disguise the intended point of attack, the quarterback must "full pivot" away from the center in order to keep his back to the defense. If his hands are big enough, he should hand the ball to the fullback and hand fake the halfback simultaneously, keeping his knees bent and weight

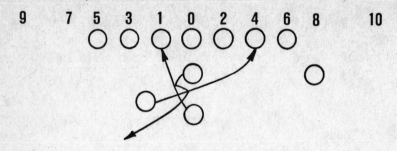

Figure 3-2

low enough to execute a good handoff and to hide behind the offensive linemen. The crossfire at four involves identical backfield action, except that the quarterback now gives the ball to the left halfback and hand fakes the fullback. Remember that these two elements in the play, the handoff and the fake, are executed simultaneously.

Depending on the fullback's speed, his alignment on the play can be from three yards to three or four feet behind the quarterback. The important point is that his positioning on this particular play be standard in order to assure a good exchange between him and the quarterback. If he cheats up too far, the quarterback may not have enough time to look the ball into his pocket. When the play is run at four and the fullback is expected to fake at one, he is told to stay tight on the quarterback in order to execute a fake good enough to hold the middle linebacker in a 6-1 or the inside linebackers in a 5-2. The halfback's responsibility is to line up approximately three yards behind the offensive tackle, straddling the tackle's inside leg. At the snap of the ball, he moves diagonally into the four hole, aiming for a spot just behind the original position of the right tackle.

These paths do not change, even if the play is a crossfire trap at four. On trap plays, to be discussed in later chapters, the halfback may have to cheat out a little, but he still moves diagonally into the four hole, staying just behind the pulling guard and favoring the double team block. The only differences in the trap play involve the fullback, who might have to fill for the pulling guard, and the quarterback, who must be especially careful not to have too much depth at the exchange. If he gets too much depth, he will force the halfback off his path and into the hole too late.

Crossfires at five and six and crossfire traps at five and six involve fundamentally the same backfield execution, with some minor adjustments in the halfback's path. The same is true when the play is run at seven or eight, although we have not used crossfire action at seven or eight, primarily because we have plays from other series that attack the outside much more effectively.

Clearly, the effectiveness of any one of these plays is dependent upon the effectiveness of the others, including the ever-present potential for additional misdirection. As is the case with all misdirection offenses, the variations in any series, if purposefully designed and well-integrated, provide not only well-sequenced alternatives but also reinforcement for the basic plays within that series. As you will see in later chapters, the potential for running the wingback on a counter play back to the five hole when the backfield is lined up in a "T 8" formation helps establish the explosiveness of a crossfire at one. The complementary relationship which exists between misdirection and the basic plays in a series constitutes one of its greatest strengths.

Much of the foregoing description has been quite detailed. This has been done by design. We learned long ago that exact explanations are necessary if our players are to execute our plays successfully. "Cheating" up or out a foot or entering the hole with exactly the right path often spells the difference between a "no gainer" and a "big gainer."

A Simple Double Digit Play

Many football teams, especially in high school, continue to use the 5-2 defense, only with a myriad of loops, slants, blitzes, and scrape-offs. If a team stunts the noseman in the 5-2 or uses him with either of the linebackers to scrape-off on the inside, the "T 8—Crossfire at 10" is a good call. The crossfire at ten tells the fullback to get a little more depth in the backfield, to start out initially at the one hole, and, after he receives the ball from the quarterback, to take an ad-justed path right at the center. The center is instructed to take the noseman any way he wants to go; the fullback will read his block and then expect to break an arm tackle if the linebacker is scraping. Obviously, the play is mirrored when "T 7—Crossfire at 20" is called.

Basic crossfire action is not a dramatic example of misdirection. It is simple and quick-hitting, but it is, at least momentarily, immobilizing for the defense. If the defense is a 6-1, crossfire action holds the middle linebacker for the critical split second needed to break a halfback through an off-tackle hole. If the defense is a 5-2, the fullback's path more than compensates for a stunting noseman, and the play hits so explosively behind either of the guards that it guaran-tees good short yardage.

Troubles? Wing It!

Crossfire action generally is very effective from any backfield set. A good way, however, to coax a defense into a particularly vulnerable position is to run Crossfire action out of the Wing formation. Look at Figure 3-3. The formation is a "Wing 8." The play is a crossfire at five. Because the Wing formation creates an offensive imbalance on one side of the line of scrimmage, it generally requires some kind of defen-sive adjustment, especially if the offense is successful run-ning to the strong side. Once the defense adjusts, a crossfire at five, a crossfire option pitch at seven, or any one of the counter traps can be very effective. These latter plays will be discussed at length in later chapters. If the defense does not adjust its alignment or its maneuvers to the strength of the offensive formation, power sweeps, quarterback rollouts, or any of several plays which capitalize on the skills of your best backs will be effective.

The point to be made here is that the potential for misdirection not only prevents your opponent from "ganging up" on defense to stop your favorite basic plays but also causes him to think twice about adjusting his defense to the

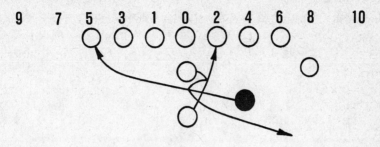

"Wing 8—Crossfire at 5"

Figure 3-3

obvious strengths of your offensive formations. He simply is unable to trust you. Each time he adjusts to the strength of a formation and you misdirect with success back to the weak side, he has to seriously question the validity of his judgment. And no one loses football games like an introspective football coach, fraught with self-doubt. Or, for that matter, no one experiences more frustration than a coach who chases up and down the sideline like the mad hatter, seeking the right combination but always guessing wrong. Misdirection can do just that to your opponents, especially if you master the "when" of its use.

Another Dimension? Try the "I"

We do not run much crossfire action from the straight "I" or from the "I" with a wing or a slotback. The "I" formation already suggests an element of unpredictability, so most defenses tend to play it pretty straight, unless the offense's tendencies have become obvious to everyone but the offense! We do run a lot of corssfire action from the "I right" and the "I left" formations. Refer to Figure 3-4. The formation is an "I right." Its mirror would be an "I left." The play diagrammed is a "Wham at 4—Isolate" versus the 5-2. The wham play obviously involves no misdirection. It is a straight-ahead power play that capitalizes on three double-team blocks and is used almost exclusively for second or third downs and short yardage. It has been one of our *most* successful plays and, as a matter of fact, has been so steady for us that we have used it often on fourth down and short yardage, even deep in our own territory. In the past, before we successfully integrated misdirection into our offense, whenever we lined up in an "I right" teams expected the "Wham at 4." They even began to cheat the noseman into the gap between our center and right guard and to stunt both linebackers into our four hole.

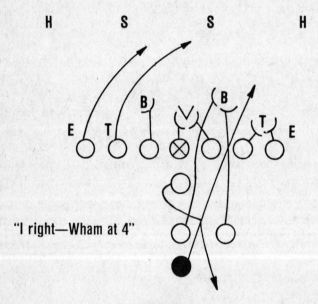

"I right—Wham at 4"

Figure 3-4

Once we mastered misdirection, we could not have been more pleased. Although our wham play was stopped momentarily, the obvious adjustments made by the defense opened up our "I Right-Crossfire at 3/Wham Action" play. Look at Figure 3-5. The backfield set is the same, and if called on a third or fourth and short yardage situation, the intent appears obvious. We even have had backs point to the four hole before the ball was snapped, then run the crossfire at three. The execution is simple. The fullback is diving at the two hole anyway; the left halfback (in the tailback position) simply hesitates a count or until the right halfback clears, and then fakes the wham into the four hole. The quarterback reverse opens instead of opening directly into the fullback, as he normally would do.

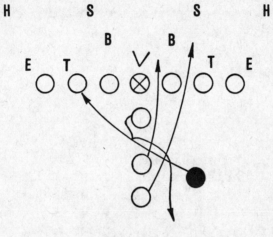

Figure 3-5

The best fake I ever saw involved a halfback who eventually became a fullback at Notre Dame. After the quarterback removed his hand from the runner's stomach, the faking halfback dove over a submarining defensive tackle. The fake attracted so much attention that the ball carrier wasn't noticed by most of the defensive team until one of the safety's tackled him in the secondary—after an eleven yard gain.

Both linebackers had moved to their left, and the noseman already had committed himself to our two hole. The crossfire at three was a natural, and, along with a few other variations, it has remained so for the past several years. This kind of misdirection play does two things for us. One, it provides an alternative to one of our favorite plays, an alternative that has earned a high degree of its own popularity, especially when the defensive adjustments give it to us. Two, it has become such a good gainer that most teams hesitate to adjust defensively. Their failure to adjust gives us the "Wham at 4" again. Misdirection either keeps them honest or forces them to guess. If they guess right, we have to rely on good execution to pick up the needed yardage. If they guess wrong, we pick up big yardage. Any time a defense is forced to guess, sooner or later they do two things. One, they admit that they can't figure you out; two, they guess wrong. Both are advantages to the offense.

Blocking the 5-2 and the 6-1

This chapter discussed the basics of the Crossfire series. As every good fundamentalist is aware, the basics must be mastered before any athlete, any technique, or any offensive system can be refined. Though these "straight-ahead" plays are basic within the crossfire series, the blocking schemes can be as sophisticated as we want or need them to be. Over the years we have developed a wide variety of blocking schemes, primarily to respond to the increasing complexity of stunting defenses. Most of these blocking schemes will be diagrammed and discussed in subsequent chapters. For now, however, and by way of introducing the need to block even your most fundamental plays in a variety of different ways, we will illustrate the same play blocked two different ways. Look at Figures 3-6 and 3-7. The formation is a "T 7." The play is a crossfire at 3. Figure 3-6 illustrates straight blocking versus the 5-2.

When the defense plays us straight up, which is a rarity, we will block them straight up, but only when we cannot afford to make a mistake or if we have the opponent overpowered, which is another rarity. Like most good offensive teams, we like to hit the same hole a number of different ways with a number of different blocking schemes. That way defensive personnel are never really sure where the ball *or* the block is coming from. Unpredictability is an important element in the techniques as well as the offensive strategies of most football teams.

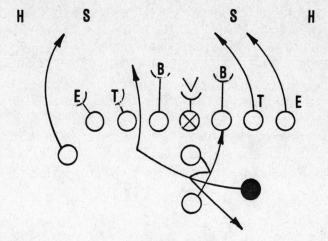

Figure 3-6

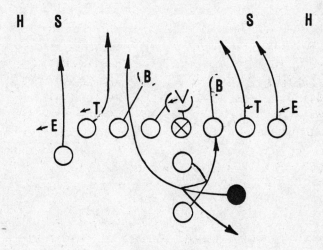

Figure 3-7

One way to vary our blocking schemes is illustrated in Figure 3-7. We have learned that some teams like to slant their defensive linemen to the wide side of the field. If we fail to adjust our blocking schemes, especially against a slanting 5-2, the noseman can do a pretty good job stopping us up the middle. "Finessing" the defensive tackle has worked well for us. He is slanting away from the point of attack anyway, and the double team block on the noseman neutralizes him. In addition, the fullback's fake holds both linebackers momentarily, long enough for the left tackle to make his block on the inside linebacker. We also have found that the tackle's block, when combined with the double team block on the noseman, often catches the offside linebacker in "the wash." The element of misdirection in the Crossfire series provides just enough unpredictability to make this play work.

Figures 3-8 and 3-9 provide additional examples of straight blocking versus finesse blocking, this time against the 6-1. The formation again is a "T 7." The play is a crossfire at 5. The wide side of the field is to the offense's left, and the assumption is that the defense will slant into the wingback.

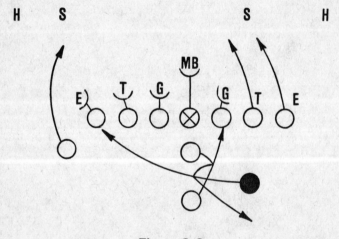

Figure 3-8

Again, the misdirection within the crossfire series is most important to the effectiveness of the play. The fullback's fake holds the middle linebacker for a split second, just long enough to give the right halfback an "extra-step" jump when he hits the five hole. The right defensive end, having outside responsibility, is unlikely to tackle the right halfback, especially if the halfback favors the double team block on the defensive tackle. This blocking scheme is very effective. Others, some equally effective, will be discussed in later chapters.

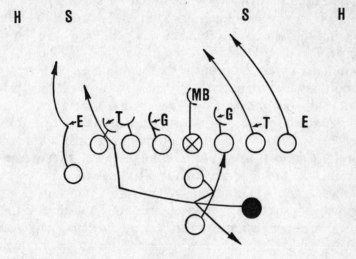

Figure 3-9

Let's Wrap It Up

As a basic series, crossfire action provides an excellent foundation for the addition of more refined plays, specifically traps, bootlegs, and counter plays. Because its basic effectiveness and the element of misdirection it involves constantly keep defenses off guard, it also provides a good basis for play-action passes. Defenses generally seem so concerned with the location of the ball on running action that they are caught flat-footed when the ball is thrown, especially on first downs or second down and short yardage.

Most importantly, crossfire action is easily introduced into your system. It involves deception, primarily the kind that only misdirection provides, but its execution is quite simple. All that is required is that the backs listen carefully to their responsibilities and execute them exactly as directed. Precision is a key word in the execution of all offensive plays but especially in the crossfire series and, most notably, with other, more sophisticated, forms of misdirection.

Finally, we provided in this chapter a brief introduction to one of our several blocking schemes. The concept of finesse blocking seems to fly in the face of all that's logical, let alone *dear*, to a football coach. Most of us have been thoroughly grounded in the philosophy that emphasizes, "If he's near the ball, knock him down." That philosophy still has its place in football, but currently we're finding that a little finesse can get the job done, too, oftentimes with a minimum of hassle. If we take the time to determine defensive tendencies, we might as well use that knowledge as another weapon, a particularly effective one, in our offensive aresenal. So, if the defensive tackle is slanting away from the point of attack, logic would dictate that we let him go. That kind of logic is even more convincing when we decide to trap him. A finessed tackle is a confused tackle. How might he feel and how might he get caught the next time when he thinks he's being finessed only to discover that he has been trapped?

This last example serves as a good summary for this chapter, and the emphasis is nothing new. But it is important. *Keep 'em guessing.* Defenses really don't like to *guess;* they like to *predict.* Take away what they like, and they're not having any fun. When they don't have fun, they lose.

4

Crossfire Traps: More Ways to Keep 'Em Guessing

The "What" and the "Why"

Trap plays have been among the biggest gainers in our offense. They are executed easily and provide an important dimension for blocking strategy. Whereas finesse blocking is most effective when the defensive line is slanting or looping in some kind of predictable fashion, trap blocking is useful when the defensive line is hard-charging and penetrates more than a foot or two beyond the line of scrimmage, *as well as* when it slants or loops. For that reason, trap blocks often are good "game openers." During that first play from scrimmage, everyone on the field is pumped up, but no one higher than the linemen, who are eager to establish the game's "pecking order." At one time or another, every lineman has been told "to go out there and prove who's boss, and he'll be 'in your pocket' for the rest of the game." It's a good principle. And it usually works.

But the "keep 'em guessing" principle works, too. It will so confuse defensive personnel that their desire to gain preeminence "in the trenches" will lose itself in momentary hesitation. They will spend much of their time trying to determine where the block is coming from, especially if the trap is used early in the game, the one time when the aggressiveness of defensive linemen is supposed to work in their favor. And it will make matters worse for defensive tackles if the next trap comes from the wingback. If untouched during the initial part of the play, a good defensive lineman has been taught to "think trap": to "look to the inside for the trapping guard" and to "make a pile" at the point of attack.

With a diversified offense attack, characterized by a variety of blocking schemes, teams can use such standard defensive principles to their own advantage. From any winged position, halfbacks, especially those who have learned to block the outside on a power sweep, can be excellent trappers. Defensive tackles who have been coached to look to the inside are easy targets for the wingback trap. And the technique is an excellent "ego booster" for the halfbacks, who generally don't get the chance to "unload" on a defensive tackle, especially when he isn't looking. Obviously, this is not a technique to be used often during a game. Once or twice is often enough. Used too frequently, the technique becomes predictable, and predictability is a bad word in football, especially for the halfback who has to trap an alerted defensive tackle. A crossfire wingback trap at 4 will be illustrated later in the chapter.

A final trap technique which has been very successful for us is the tackle trap. Already discussed briefly in earlier chapters, the tackle trap is used by us exclusively with counter plays. This is not to say that it can't be used with other kinds of trap plays. We simply never have had the exceptionally fast tackle in combination with the delayed backfield action that is required to use the tackle in a routine trap play. The tackle trap, however, is an excellent strategy with counter plays, primarily because it provides no key for the inside linebackers. Tackle traps, because they relate in our offense exclusively to counter plays, will be illustrated and discussed in Chapter 5.

Simple Traps Within the Crossfire Series

The basic traps within the series are the Crossfire Traps at 3,4,5, and 6. The traps at 3 and 4 are most effective against the 5-2 or any other odd front; the traps at 5 and 6 are best against the 6-1. The traps at 3 or 4 versus the 5-2 provide three important advantages. One, they provide for a double-team block on a particularly talented noseguard. Two, they provide for the double team block on the noseguard who may not be particularly talented but who slants, along with the rest of the defensive line, in a random, unpredictable way and who seems invariably to find his way into the backfield. Three, it provides the angle for the tackle to "down block" the onside linebacker, who already has been delayed by the fullback's fake. Refer to Figure 4-1. The formation is a "T 8." The play is a crossfire trap at 4 versus the 5-2.

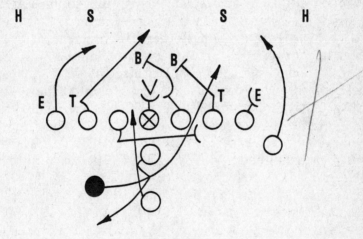

Figure 4-1

Backfield Action

The backfield action is basically the same as the regular crossfire at four. The one exception is that the half-back, depending upon his speed, is instructed to cheat out one to two feet to maintain proper distance from the trapping

guard. He doesn't want to beat the guard to the point of
attack. Nor does he want to get there late. So we instruct the
quarterback to take the ball to the halfback and to avoid any
depth in the backfield. If the quarterback gets too much
depth, he'll push the running back off his path. A proper path
should result in a diagonal entry into the four hole.

Many coaches might disagree with this angle of entry,
especially on trap plays. Many feel that the halfback should
move parallel to the line of scrimmage during his initial few
steps, then plant and cut vertically into the four hole. These
coaches argue that such an entry "sets up" the tackle for the
guard's trap block. We have found that most tackles don't
pay much attention to the offside back, especially if the
tackle's responsibility is to keep the offensive lineman off the
linebackers. He's watching for movement from the nearest
opponent, the guy who is breathing fire directly across from
him. In addition, current defensive philosophies and techniques pre-commit most defensive linemen. The defensive
call directs them to slant, to veer, to submarine, to loop, or to
execute any one of a number of techniques that confuse
offensive blocking schemes. Because the defensive linemen
are generally pre-committed, we have found that a quicker
hitting play is much more effective, so we move the halfback
diagonally into the four hole from his home position.

The crossfire trap at 5 or 6, particularly versus the 6-1,
involves a halfback path which more nearly approximates
parallel action. Refer to Figure 4-2. Because the play hits an
off-tackle hole, the halfback may be expected to follow a
parallel path, at least initially. One reason involves his *not*
wanting to hit the hole before the guard gets there. A second
involves his wanting to make the defensive end very conscious of his outside responsibility. Defensive ends in the 6-1
and outside backers *do* key backfield action, generally the
movements of the back farthest from them. If the defensive
end slides to the outside or "boxes" to face up with backfield
action, he is very "trappable." The halfback's path should
encourage the defensive end to protect the outside. If the end
disregards the halfback's path by sensing a trap play and
reacting hard to shut down the off-tackle hole, the crossfire

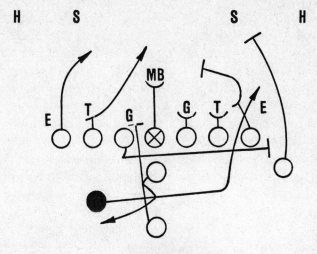

Figure 4-2

option at 7 or 8 is a good call. Because it involves a "guard off pull" and serves to complement the crossfire trap at 5 and 6, the option play will be diagrammed and discussed in a later section of this chapter.

Attacking the 5-2 with a 12 Trap

This has been a big play for us. We have been blessed with several excellent fullbacks, who have developed a good "feel" for the play and have mastered its execution. Conversely, the strategic effectiveness of the play makes it so successful that the fullbacks like to run it. They soon realize that they have a good chance of making big yardage if they run it correctly. The 12 or 21 trap is perhaps our most successful double digit play. As a quick reminder, double digit plays involve a path for the ball carrier which starts him in one direction, then veers him in another. We might call it "one-man misdirection."

Refer to Figure 4-3. The formation, again, is a T 8. For purposes of illustration, it could have been any one of several formations. Coaches interested in using this play will determine the formation based upon the pattern of their offense

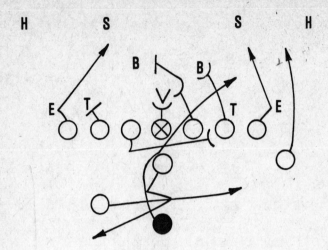

Figure 4-3

and any weaknesses they observe on the defense. For purposes of illustration, however, the T 8 is as good as any other.
The 12 trap starts the fullback toward the left guard (the one
hole), then veers him toward the right guard (the two hole).
One and two, for us double-digit coaches, equals 12.

Aside from the fullback's path and the fact that the play
involves a trap, the primary differences between the 12 trap
and a regular crossfire at one involve the fullback's initial
alignment and the point of exchange. Because the fullback
must give the guard time to make his trap block and the
tackle time to get the linebacker, especially versus the 6-1, he
is instructed to line up four to five yards behind the quarterback. The quarterback is instructed to take the ball *back* to
the fullback. Obviously, they meet somewhere in between,
but the point of exchange is still deep enough to give the
fullback time to make his cut and to hit the point of attack
somewhere between the center and offensive right guard.

To avoid an obvious key, the halfbacks are instructed to
get depth, too, almost as much as the fullback. Even with
this adjustment, the 12 trap still might provide an excellent
key for the defense were it not for the fact that the fullback is
instructed to get similar depth in many of the counter plays.
For that matter, the fullback can camouflage his depth in the

12 trap by getting depth in other series when he is not moving the ball or making a key block. This observation simply reinforces the fact that "the day of the dumb football player is over." Fullbacks, along with every other player on the team, have a great deal to think about during the course of a football game.

The Line

The line splits for this play are routine: two to three feet for each of the linemen. The double team block on the noseman is critical. The initial execution of the block is no different from any other double team block. The center is expected to "post" the noseman by sticking his forehead on the numbers, and the right guard is expected to "drive" him away from the point of attack with a near head and shoulder block. The focal element in this part of the play involves the noseman's initial move. If he is pre-committed to slant or loop to his right, away from the guard's drive block, we instruct the guard to pass by him and go to the "next plateau." For purposes of this play, the next plateau is the offside linebacker.

He is instructed to do so for two important reasons. One, we don't want to waste him on a noseman who is stunting himself out of the play. Two, which is somewhat more important, we will have to adjust to one of several defensive stunts which could result from the noseman's initial move. First, the entire defensive line might be slanting to their right. If this is the case, the left guard's trap block at four is going to be difficult. The defensive left tackle probably will be slanting into the four hole, so the play will probably end up at two or even zero. The guard's block on the offside linebacker, therefore, is very important, because the play will be run much closer to the linebacker. Second, the offside linebacker might be "scraping" with the noseman. See Figure 4-4. The right guard's block on the offside linebacker becomes even more important, because the linebacker's stunt will take him right to the point of attack.

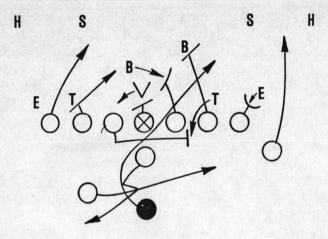

Figure 4-4

Getting to the Linebacker

Two more points are important for the proper execution of the play. The offensive right guard's block on the onside linebacker is the most important part of the play. Because most defensive maneuvers are designed to keep the offensive linemen off the linebackers, the right tackle should expect contact from the lineman in front of him, especially if the defensive lineman has been directed to slant hard to his right. For that reason, we instruct our linemen, in this instance our offensive right tackle, to make hard contact with the man in front of them, *then* to move to the linebacker. An offensive tackle who tries to "sneak by" a defensive tackle rarely will get to a linebacker. He either will be knocked down by the defensive tackle or will be knocked off his path sufficiently to be unable to make good contact with the linebacker. Having made the contact to guarantee his balance, the offensive tackle should move quickly to the onside linebacker.

The momentary delay which results from the tackle's contact with the defensive lineman also assists with the strategic effectiveness of the play. If not blocked immediately, most linebackers will focus all their attention on the ball carrier, expecting to execute a crowd-pleasing form tackle. The tackle's block almost always catches the line-backer by surprise. And it comes at exactly the right time. The fullback's initial depth and his adjusted path delay the play just long enough to give the tackle time enough to get to the linebacker, usually just before the fullback gets there. We have never seen him get there too late. Once the tackle eliminates the onside backer, the fullback has a clear path to the onside safety, who is likely to be preoccupied with the wingback's block and the halfback's fake.

The second important point involves the fullback's path. All running backs on all plays must know where their blocks are coming from. They also must read defensive stunts. The 12 trap requires that the fullback read the noseman's initial movements. Once the noseman stunts to his right, essentially out of the play, the fullback must expect pressure from the offside linebacker or from the defensive left tackle. His primary block, however, will come from his right tackle. The right tackle's block is the key that will open the play.

It Hurts the 6-1, Too

The 12 trap also is effective versus the 6-1. See Figure 4-5. Obviously, the backfield action is the same. So is the line blocking, with the exception of a blocking scheme which we call "Exit" blocking to enable the tackle to get to the middle linebacker. If the quarterback observes a 6-1 defense instead of a 5-2 as the offense approaches the line of scrimmage, he calls out "Exit" before he starts his cadence. The call instructs the linemen at the point of attack, in this case the right guard and tackle, to exit block the man on the head of the offensive tackle. The guard's block on the defensive tackle accomplishes two things. One, it frees the offensive tackle to block the middle linebacker. Two, the right guard's "out move" causes the defensive guard to lean to *his* outside, setting up the left guard's trap block.

The quarterback calls the blocking scheme to avoid giving the defense any clues as to where the offense plans to run the ball. Some teams have the tackles designate the blocking schemes at the line of scrimmage. We have dis-

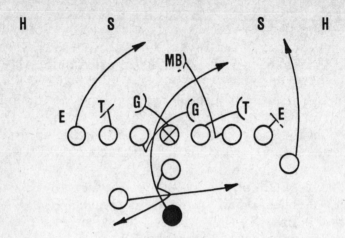

Figure 4-5

covered that we'd rather not play that game. When our
tackles called the blocking schemes, we also had to have
them give a phoney call when they were not involved in the
blocking at the point of attack. Often they would forget, or at
times they would provoke the defense into a stunt which
either confused the blocking scheme or prevented them from
getting downfield to block. When the quarterback started
making the call, we were assured that the responsibility
rested with one man, usually one who was very involved in
the game, and that the absence of clues would cause the
defense to play us pretty straight. And that's what happened.

The 12 trap or its mirror, the 21 trap, is an excellent
football play. It doesn't involve any razzle dazzle, just good
hard fundamentals as well as the basic simplicity which
characterizes most good strategy. We have used it often and
will continue to do so. Our opponents know that we use it,
but because it complements our offense so well, they don't
know when we will use it. And, like all other misdirection
plays, it looks like one of our basic plays, especially at the
snap of the ball.

Consider Another Option

The triple option and the Houston Veer are probably the top two option series in football today. Both emphasize the "keep 'em guessing" principle, and each requires a careful study of defensive assignments and tendencies in order to sequence properly. The inside belly option, similar in design to the triple option, is probably our best option play. A good fake by the fullback at three or four can immobilize almost any defense, especially the linebackers and the secondary. But the crossfire option, because it complements much of our trap action, is essential within our offensive attack. Look at Figure 4-6. As indicated earlier in this chapter, the initial execution of the crossfire option at 8 is initially identical to the crossfire trap at 6. More importantly, the crossfire option, unlike most option plays, puts the defensive end (the outside man on the line of scrimmage for those of you who might call him an outside backer) in a double bind. One, he has the responsibility of reading and reacting to the quarterback's option. Two, if he reacts to the quarterback, he has the

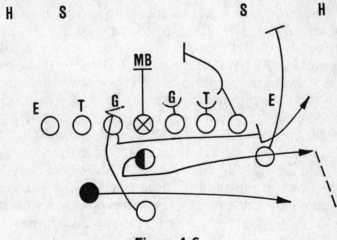

Figure 4-6

pulling guard to contend with. Assume that he reacts to the quarterback and gets cut down by the pulling guard. The quarterback still can keep the ball to the outside and option the defensive halfback. If the defensive end covers the pitch-back, a defensive assignment which is more likely, the quarterback can turn up field, the pulling guard leading the way for him.

A few comments about execution are necessary. At the snap, the quarterback opens into the fullback, ball fakes him, and then hesitates one half count. The hesitation is needed to give the pulling left guard time to clear the center. The quarterback then pivots, looking immediately at the defensive end and finding the pitchback peripherally. From that point his execution is similar to that of most other option plays. Like the quarterback, the pulling guard has a responsibility of finding the defensive end immediately. The defensive end is his primary responsibility. If the end comes hard, the guard is instructed to cut him down. If the end covers the pitchback, the guard is instructed to turn up field and block for the quarterback, looking to the inside for immediate pressure.

The option, like the crossfire trap at 5 or 6, seems to be most effective against the 6-1, although we have used it very successfully against the 5-2. Against the 5-2, the fullback's fake must hold both linebackers. Normally, however, only one is keying him, so at times his fake is wasted. And, unless a linebacker is blitzing, he has no one to block when filling for the pulling guard. If his fake is ignored, however, we have an excellent pass play off option action to use. The play will be diagrammed and discussed in Chapter 8.

Against the 6-1, the fullback has a defensive guard to block. In addition, the initial part of his fake will hold the middle linebacker, who almost always has the fullback as his key. To compound the middle linebacker's dilemma, both the center and the right guard are blocking him.

Try an Occasional Wingback Trap

As mentioned earlier in this chapter, the wingback trap can keep defensive tackles guessing throughout most of the game. Look at Figure 4-7. The play is a crossfire wingback trap at 6 versus the 5-2. In order to avoid confusion for the offensive linemen, the blocking assignments are identical to the regular crossfire trap at 4. The only difference involves the left guard and the wingback. The left guard is directed to "inside release" past the linebacker on his head and to cut down the onside safety. The wingback is instructed to block the defensive tackle, who, because of his training, is likely to be looking to the inside for the guard trap. Because the left defensive end normally has outside responsibility, the offensive right end is instructed to shoulder block him initially and then slide into a crab block to prevent his recovery to the off tackle hole.

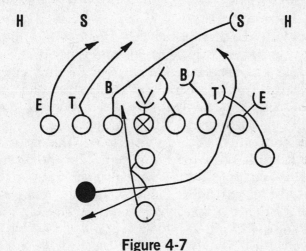

Figure 4-7

Because the wingback's initial move simulates counter action, it tends to freeze the defensive left halfback, who usually has an "outside-in" pursuit path anyway. If the fullback's fake can hold the offside linebacker and if the left guard can at least shield the onside safety, the play is a good ground gainer. As with the regular guard trap at 6, the right guard is instructed to double-team block the noseman. If the noseman is taken by the center or if he stunts himself away from the action, the right guard will go to the "next plateau," the offside linebacker.

The blocking scheme is fundamentally sound. It should be used, however, only occasionally. A steady diet of the wingback trap can be very unhealthy for the wingback. The fundamental purpose of the wingback trap is to keep the defensive tackle guessing. It is designed to introduce a blocking variation. If used in conjunction with the guard trap and the finesse block, the defensive tackle will never really be sure where the block is coming from. A good wingback trap, if used only once, will make the tackle nervous the next time he is being finessed. He is likely to be conscious of the wingback while the ball carrier is running right by him.

Let's Wrap It Up

Two kinds of trap plays were introduced in this chapter. A third, the tackle trap, will become the focus of the next chapter. Trap plays, especially when used in conjunction with misdirection, can be very effective strategically, in spite of the obvious keys they provide. Because most linebackers look through the guards to their backfield keys, guard traps normally provide good clues at to where the offense intends to run the ball. Many defensive guards in the 6-1 and most inside linebackers in the 5-2 will start their pursuit paths as soon as the guard pulls. For that matter, many defensive guards, especially if they have good speed, will *follow* the guard. Some will follow so quickly that the fullback who is filling for the guard will be unable to stop him. If the defensive guard is quick, and many of them are, he can cause all kinds of problems in the backfield.

The best way we know to keep him honest is to "influence pull" the left guard and to give the fullback the ball at the one hole. See Figure 4-8. The play is identical to the crossfire at six, with the exception that the fullback is carrying the ball at one. Although the influence pull is especially effective against a defensive guard who is cheating, the strategy also is effective against a 5-2 linebacker who cheats by pursuing as soon as he sees the guard pull. But the

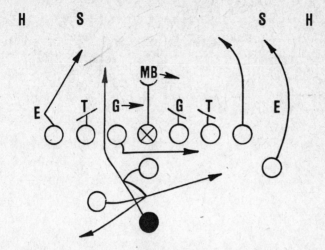

Figure 4-8

strategy is particularly good versus the 6-1 because the defensive guard is keying only the man in front of him. Even if he fails to follow the guard, he has no clue that the fullback has the ball. In essence, the defensive guard is "finessed."

Versus the 5-2, the inside linebackers key *through* the guards to the backfield. Even though the guard pulls, the linebacker may still see that his key has the ball. The primary reason underlying the use of the influence pull, however, is to prevent the defender from cheating by embarrassing him. Again, the strategy is to be used only once or twice during a game, if that much. Someone will have to determine that the defender is cheating, and then the influence pull will have to be called, but at such a time that a mistake will not seriously affect the outcome of the game. The purpose of the influence pull is not to make big yardage but to keep the defensive guard or linebacker honest. Like the wingback trap, a steady diet of running at an influence pull can make for a very unhealthy situation for the fullback.

Basic, double digit, and wingback traps within the Crossfire series are very effective, primarily because of the misdirection the series provides. It is momentarily immobilizing for the defense and presents, from the same formation, a variety of attack points as well as blocking schemes along the line of scrimmage. The tackle trap, as used with the counter play, provides the final dimension for the team to diversify the method as well as the execution of its offensive attack. Counter plays will be discussed in the next two chapters.

5

The Counter Play:
Making Good Use
of the Tackle

O.K., let's talk some more *football* and continue to avoid the sand lot razzle dazzle. Some authors seem to push razzle dazzle in the name of "new," and many of us often make the mistake of thinking that "new" means "better." So encouraged, many would-be theorists throw a myriad of complex plays at us and execute them from such elaborate formations that only a chess master can understand them. And we dutifully discard the series that we have toiled over for years. The basic series that we have developed can still work, regardless of their age and of the "better" concepts being thrown at us. Add a little misdirection to your basic series, and as the saying goes, "they've not grown older; they've grown better."

With the possible exception of our formation calling system, much of what we have discussed thus far represents little more than a new wrinkle on some successful but old ideas. These old ideas, especially with the new wrinkles, really work. We tend to remain with the more conventional ways of doing things, not because we are stuck in an

71

uncreative rut or have a blind reverence for the past, but because we have discovered that genuine creativity requires a knowledge of the past and a fresh insight into the good that it represented. We've discovered that we do not need fancy formations or schoolyard gimmicks to be creative. Creative football, like any other art, requires a thorough knowledge of what you're doing.

Counter plays are creative. They do not require the complete overhaul of your system, just a few minor tune-ups that will complement what you already do best. Having made a relatively inexpensive investment in the system by adding counters with the tackle trap, you'll find that it not only works and looks better but gives you more mileage. Following are only a few advantages.

Counters Are Exciting

Nothing pleases a crowd more than the surprise of discovering the ball in the hands of a back who seemed to pop out of nowhere. And nothing frustrates a defense more. Just imagine the bewildered defensive halfback, watching the organized confusion before him, then suddenly realizing that the ball carrier is right on top of him. The crowd appeal of such plays rests on this element of confusion, because the confusion results in defensive mis-cues and, in effect, paves the way for big ground gainers. Quick openers and routine power sweeps, even though at times they may pick up fairly good yardage, satisfy the knowledgeable football fan. But all those mothers and girlfriends who think that Johnny looks cute in his uniform need a little something else to catch their attention. Even many of the dads respect and appreciate the excitement of a well-executed counter play. A team that runs misdirection remains unpredictable, a fact which presents a threat to the opposing team and a sense of anticipation to the fans. The experience is reminiscent of Mickey Mantle during his heyday with the Yankees. The pitcher and the fans all knew that he would do whatever was strategically necessary to win the game. But everyone waited anxiously because they knew that one swing of the bat might send a pitch out of the ball park.

Counters Are Precise

Counters are the running game's equivalent of sending one out of the ball park. But, like Mantle's swing of the bat, they require precision. And precision comes from practice. We time all our counter plays for at least fifteen minutes a day, excluding the time we scrimmage with them. The players sometimes get a little bored with the repetition, but they stay with it without too much "prompting" on our part. They realize, especially after a game or two, how important the counters are to our offensive attack.

As you will notice later on in this chapter, counter plays result in players running "every which way." The tackle and the wingback are moving counter to backfield flow. One or more fakes are executed before the hand off. The fullback is filling for the pulling tackle. To be executed effectively, this kind of play requires split-second timing. If only one thing goes wrong, the fullback bumping into the pulling tackle, for example, the play is dead. So be sure to schedule enough time in each practice session to develop the precision required to execute each play well.

The Team Will Believe in Them

Even before your first game, the team will have confidence in the effectiveness of its counter plays. Everyone will have a chance to observe them in practice. The eagerness of the defensive players, especially those young ones who are anxious to make the team, parallels the aggressiveness of a hard-charging defensive line on game days. When combined with the inexperience of the young players during pre-season scrimmages, the element of misdirection convinces the offensive team that counter plays really work—and they do. With this kind of initial exposure to the success of the counter play, the team will be well-induced to commit the time and energy needed to continue to perfect them well into the season.

Another advantage accrues to the coaching staff. The team also believes in *them*. A coach who can diagram a well-conceived counter play, develop the drills to make it work, and evidence the strategic knowledge to call it at the right time must have "moxey." Clearly, many other factors contribute to the success of a football coach. But if he can command the respect of his players and make the season exciting as well as successful, he is well on his way to having his players believe in him.

So Will the Defense

The opposing team will believe in him, too. But it won't be as much fun for them. They will learn early in the game to mistrust their defensive keys. The onside safety who keys the home halfback and leaves his position in hot pursuit is the perfect target for a counter play. His key will remove him from the point of attack, and nothing is more frustrating for a hard-nosed safety than to be running in one direction while the ball carrier is observed running in another. Not only will this cause mistrust of keys, but it will also re-establish the strength of your basic series by immobilizing defensive personnel.

Be careful, however, when using counter plays against a team that also uses counter plays well. Although they provide the same kind of strategic advantage, they probably cannot be used as frequently during the game. A team that uses counter plays as an essential part of their offensive attack runs them often enough so that their defense becomes able to sense them. Although the occasional use of a counter play will serve to keep that defense honest, it may not provide the game-breaking big gainer that it can provide against other defenses. Our experience has been to use the counter play against such defenses, but also to use influence pulling and our basic plays with counter action to further confuse defensive keys. We can run an option at 8 with counter action if the defensive secondary starts pursuing on the wingback's path. Look at Figure 5-1.

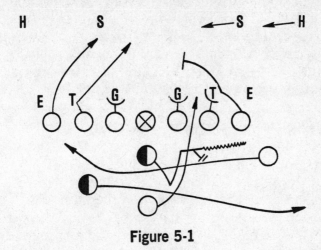

Figure 5-1

The formation is a "T 8." The play is an "inside belly option at 8/counter action." The term "counter action" refers only to the wingback, not the tackle. The tackle is responsible for executing his assignment for the option play. The "counter action" call simply instructs the wingback to move along the line of scrimmage, as he would during a regular counter play, to take a fake from the quarterback, and to continue with that fake into the line of scrimmage. If he runs into a defensive man, in essence forcing himself to be tackled, the fake will be even better.

If the defensive secondary keys the wingback and pursues on his action and if the quarterback and wingback execute good fakes, the quarterback merely has to option the end, and the play is a gainer. The play is especially illusive if the offensive right end can pass up the double-team block with the tackle and "plateau" to the linebacker. His initial movement will then simulate a downfield blocking path and will provide yet another misleading key for the secondary.

To repeat an important point, counter plays and counter action provide the important dimension of hitting almost every hole along the line of scrimmage from the same formation with the same backfield action. "Counter action" also reinforces the principle that it may be better to fake out two men than to block one. With this kind of strategy, even against a team that also runs the counter play, they'll continue to believe in you, not so much because of your execution of the counter play but because of that little nuisance, unpredictability.

An Aid to the Passing Game

Imagine the defensive secondary, especially late in the game, unsure of their defensive keys and strongly conscious of the offense's potential for counter plays. Imagine also that you have a counter action pass in your play book. Look at Figure 5-2. The play is a "Crossfire counter action pass at 7." The formation again is a "T 8." This kind of play obviously is most effective in "non-passing" situations: first and ten, second and four, and the like. The old axiom that pass plays are most effective if executed close to a first down situation is very true. The defensive secondary will be least prepared for a pass if it is thrown on a first and ten situation. They will be *most* prepared on a *third* and ten. If executed early and with play action, a good pass play can become not only a big gainer but also another element in the unpredictability of the team's offensive attack.

Execution is critical. Backfield execution must simulate the counter play. Each back must execute his fakes deliberately and well into the line of scrimmage. Perhaps the most important backfield fake involves the quarterback. He must "ball fake" each of the two "home" backs, then the wingback as the wingback executes his counter fake. If the quarterback hurries any of these fakes, especially the fake to the wingback, he won't hold the defensive secondary. The secondary's first few steps are backward anyway because of his primary responsibility to defend against the pass. The backfield action and the pass routes of the two primary receivers must immobilize the secondary, especially the safeties, one or both of whom are likely to be responsible for the deep pass.

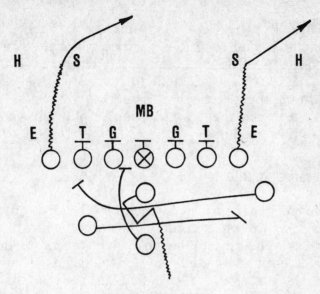

Figure 5-2

The two ends must help immobilize the secondary. Each during his first steps must forget that he is a pass reciever. Their initial responsibility is to "stalk" the safeties as if to block them. The intent is to invite the safeties toward the line of scrimmage, then streak past them on their pass routes. The tactic is very effective, especially if the ends don't commit too early and if the backfield extends its fakes long enough to help immobilize the defensive secondary.

Counter action passes, as with all play action passes, represent one phase of the offensive attack. Counter plays are not run to set up the counter action pass, although they do. Nor is the counter action pass thrown to set up the counter plays, although it does. The important aspect of the relationship between running and passing plays, as with misdirection and the basic offense, is its complementarity. All elements of an effective offensive attack are essentially equal, the effectiveness of each dependent upon how each is executed and when each is called.

Counter plays, then, serve to add yet another dimension to a team's offensive effectiveness. Not only do they threaten the defense, but they provide a source of confidence for the team and an added element of excitement for the fans. They also require precision and split-second timing. But their effectiveness as a complement to the rest of the offensive attack more than compensates for the time and energy required to make them work. Counter plays are not only effective; they are fun.

The Crossfire Counter

The crossfire counter may be more fun than any of the counter plays we run. It certainly is one of the most exciting to watch as well as one of the most confusing for the defense. Its excitement and its confusion for the defense result from the total effect of its execution. Everybody seems to be moving in a different direction. That fact seems to be the single most important characteristic underlying the effectiveness of the crossfire counter. The misdirection within the backfield action, the wingback's movement parallel to the line of scrimmage, the tackle's pulling, and the fullback's adjusted path to fill for the tackle all combine to create a "tangle" of movement. The cumulative effect of all the movement becomes immobilizing for the defense. Refer to Figures 5-3 and 5-4.

You already know the formation. The play is a "crossfire counter at 5" versus both the 6-1 and the 5-2. The play's ability to immobilize a defense relates to its movement. Consider defensive keys. The onside safety is likely to be assigned the left halfback. The middle linebacker in the 6-1 is likely to be assigned the fullback. Such defensive keys, which tend to be standard within most defenses, will move each defender away from the point of attack. The safety certainly won't leave his position as fast as we might like him to because he still has pass responsibility and will be conscious of the left end's movement toward him. But the play's simulation of either a crossfire 12 trap or a crossfire at four will tend to move the safety up and to his left. That's just where we want him.

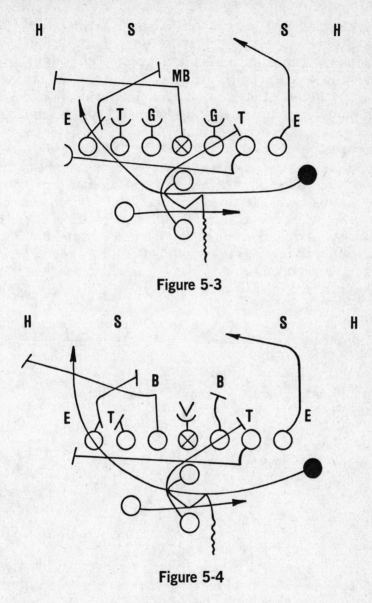

Figure 5-3

Figure 5-4

The only reliable key is the defensive right halfback's key on the offensive left end. The left end's "down block" on the defensive tackle is a clear message to the defensive halfback that the play is a likely trap at the five hole. But because he is the "last line of defense" to the outside, he normally is given an outside-in pursuit path, that is, his pursuit path on run action to his side is, first, to move to the line of scrimmage and, second, to position himself in such a way as to keep the ball carrier and the blockers to his inside in order to force the action back to the inside, back toward his pursuing teammates. The defensive end has much the same responsibility. He must always check for bootleg, counter, reverse, and screen and then force the play to his inside. We don't worry about him. There seems to be nothing more enjoyable for an offensive tackle than having the chance to trap a defensive end, especially if the end is facing up to backfield action. A good, aggressive tackle doesn't see a defensive end while coming down the line of scrimmage; he sees an unsuspecting ten pin. And after the end gets blocked, that's almost what he looks like. Unlike the defensive secondary and the defensive tackles, defensive ends are taught to face up to backfield action and to meet everything with the inside shoulder in order to force the play to the inside. Because he can't "give himself up" on the trapping tackle, he is very "blockable."

The defensive halfback is another story. Although his pursuit path is likely to remove him from the point of attack, he can cause problems for the play, especially if he is quick and reads the play well. The center's block, therefore, is very important. If the center is to get to the defensive halfback as quickly as is necessary to make the play go, the middle linebacker will have to be influenced by the backfield action, especially by the fullback, who is his primary key. If the fullback makes a good fake before he fills for the offensive right tackle, the middle linebacker should take one step first to his own right, then move quickly to his left. The center is instructed to make contact with the middle linebacker with his right shoulder and, *without stopping his legs*, to release and to take a collision path with the onside defensive halfback. The center's block is very important to the success of the play.

When Is the Best Time?

The "when" of all counter action already has been discussed in an earlier chapter, but a few reminders are necessary. The first reminder is the most important. Use the counter play when the defensive secondary begins to rotate on the action of the offensive backfield, particularly when the secondary becomes anxious about the fullback's success up the middle. The rotation of the defensive secondary is perhaps the easiest clue to find when studying the opponent's defense. Their movements and the evidence of the keys which caused them are obvious to everyone on the sidelines.

A second reminder involves the determination of the slanting techniques of the defensive line. If their slanting becomes predictable, to the long and strong side, for example, or into or away from the wingback, use counter action and the double team block it provides on the defensive tackle. This reminder suggests one reason why it is always a good idea to chart your opponent's defensive stunts. Analyzing a chart, especially at halftime, eventually will reveal a defensive tendency. Once discovered by the offense, that tendency will become an obvious but unrecognized disadvantage for the defense. The least the identification of a tendency can do is chase a defensive team out of its favorite defense and force them into something they may not like as well.

A final reminder involves down and distance. Don't call counter plays out of a sense of panic. Like pass plays, they may be quite ineffective on a third and ten situation, when the defensive secondary is dropped off anyway and the linebackers are more pass conscious. This is not to say that counters will never work on third and ten situations. A hard-charging defensive lineman, thinking little more than pass rush, is the perfect target for a trapping tackle. We have used counter plays on third and long and have used them with success. The important point to remember, however, is that if used on a second and four or a first and ten or even a third and one, you may never have a third and ten during the ball game. Counter plays may not always pick up big yardage for you, but they will keep the defense so off balance that the rest of your offense will pick up yardage more consistently.

How to Run the Crossfire Counter

Remember that counters are precise. They require timing during most practice sessions, not a lot of time but enough to impress upon the team the need for precision and the importance of being *involved* in the execution of the play. A back or a lineman who feels that his responsibility during the play is unimportant or who decides to take a little breather does so at the expense of his teammates. The play probably will not go. The execution of counter plays is so exact that every player must put forth just a little more each time one is called.

The players' sense of involvement is particularly important. With the advent of play-calling from the sidelines, we discovered several years ago that our players could not involve themselves in what was happening strategically on the field. A result was that we had to ride herd on them more and more each year. To combat this tendency, we began asking our offensive team after each series on the sidelines to diagram defensive stunts, to identify the holes to hit, and even to suggest the plays to run. Fortunately, their suggestions have been consistent with our perceptions of what we needed to do, so most of the time we have been able to use what they have recommended. And usually it has worked. But, and of most importance, their sense of involvement has had considerable carry-over value. They don't feel like robots going through the motions; they feel genuinely involved in each play that we call.

Backfield Action

The backs feel involved because they generally are more aware of the particular play to recommend, unlike the

linemen who know what holes to hit. The linemen, especially
late in the first quarter, have a pretty good idea of what they
can and cannot do to the man across from them. Once the
backs recommend the play, they feel committed to make it
go. They are willing to put forth greater effort and are more
inclined to remember and to effect the finer points of its
execution.

The crossfire counter has several fine points that need to
be remembered. Take a quick look at Figures 5-3 and 5-4
again.

The Quarterback

The quarterback's most important responsibility is to
get depth on his first two steps. First, he is to get enough
depth to allow the tackle to clear and the fullback to fill for
him. Second, he has to be deep enough so that at the
exchange of the ball the wingback is deep enough in the
backfield to make the proper entry into the five hole. The cut
is difficult enough without the additional problem of not
having adequate depth in the backfield. The counter play at
3 or 4 involves an even more difficult entry for the wingback.
Look at Figures 5-5 and 5-6. Although the play is diagrammed versus both the 5-2 and the 6-1, the counter at 3 or 4 is
particularly effective against the 5-2. The reason involves the
double-team block on the noseman and its added possibility
of catching the offside linebacker "in the wash."

Regarding the quarterback's depth, however, the counters at 3 and 4 underscore the importance of the quarterback's depth, as well as his need to "full pivot" so that the
hand-off, when the play is run at 3, occurs behind the
offensive right guard. The exchange at that point gives the
ball carrier time to concentrate on the tackle's trap and to
make the cut into the hole, which may be close to the one
hole, especially if the entire defensive line is slanting *into* the
wingback. The quarterback must be careful, though, to keep
his feet directly under his body. A foot placed too far in front
of him can trip the intended ball carrier, a mistake which

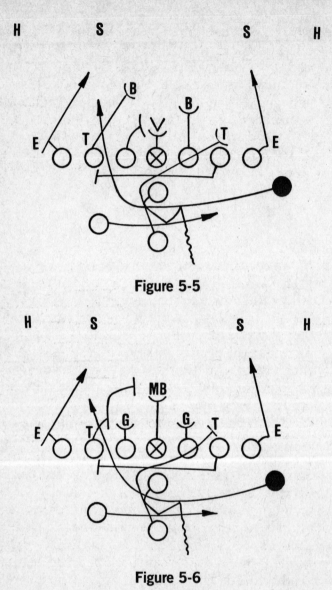

Figure 5-5

Figure 5-6

can result in not only lost yardage but a very red-faced coach on the sidelines. And the red face is likely to reflect much more than embarrassment!

A final important point involves the two fakes which precede the hand off. The basic plays within the crossfire series normally involve a simultaneous hand off and a hand fake. Because the counter play involves so much action behind and in front of the quarterback, he is instructed to *ball fake* both the fullback and the halfback before he gives the ball to the wingback. By "ball faking" each of the two home backs, the quarterback keeps two hands on the ball, assuring greater control of the ball and minimizing the possibility of a fumble. This is a fairly obvious point to a seasoned coach, but its importance, especially early in the season, makes it worth mentioning.

The Fullback

Another fairly obvious point involves the initial positioning of the fullback. If he is to make a good fake and cut early enough to get between the quarterback and pulling tackle in order to fill for him, he must get added depth as he lines up. Whereas the fullback's normal alignment is three to three and a half yards behind the quarterback, his adjusted alignment on the counter play should be at least five yards behind the quarterback. The added depth allows the quarterback room to get his drop away from the line, and it gives the fullback room in order to fill for the tackle. The extra yard and a half depth could be a good key for the defense, were it not for the fact that the home halfback is also getting added depth, a good camouflaging technique and a requirement for good execution. In addition, our offense requires the fullback to get added depth on other plays as well.

Some added mention might be made about the fullback's technique when he fakes and fills for the pulling tackle. If the center is to get free in order to block the onside defensive halfback, the fullback's fake will have to influence the linebacker(s). The linebacker in the 6-1 will have to take two to three steps away from the point of attack. If the fullback is instructed to run into the defensive tackle rather than to block him, the fake will be much more effective. All he need do is drop his inside shoulder over the quarterback's ball fake, plant his outside foot in order to be on a collision path with the defensive tackle, and then lower his shoulder into the defensive tackle. Given the fact that occasionally we will run an influence pull, the defensive tackle may go for the fullback's fake. If he does tackle the fullback, the play can be exceptionally effective. Even if the defensive tackle does not go for the fullback, the fullback is instructed to go for the tackle. If, when the fullback goes for the tackle, he drops the shoulder and hits the tackle solidly, he not only will stop the tackle's penetration but will draw a lot of attention away from the point of attack on the other side of the line. This technique simply reaffirms the notion that a fake which influences two or three defenders can be more effective than a block which may eliminate only one. Plus, the innate masochism of a good fullback makes him happy when he fakes so well that he gets tackled.

The Wingback

The original positioning of the wingback is subject to the particular counter play to be run and to the speed of the ball carrier. Early in the season we instruct all the halfbacks, when they are winged, to align themselves approximately one yard outside and one yard behind the offensive end. Again, this position will vary according to the speed and maneuverability of the winged back. Once he establishes the ideal positioning for himself, however, he should try as much as possible to standardize it on all plays in order to avoid providing a key for the defense when a counter play is to be run.

We also have discovered that a forward jab step doesn't fool anyone, especially the defensive halfback who normally is keying him and who probably will not be involved in the play anyway. We instruct the wingback to start his parallel move immediately. His balance is better, and the timing of the play is improved.

A final point involving the wingback is important. Normally, a good backfield coach does not like to tell a ball carrier where to run. He certainly will coach him regarding some of the fine points of running technique, such as lowering the shoulder and driving the legs, even setting up his blocks and spinning out of a tackle. But normally he will not establish a steady diet of telling the player where to go on every play. It's just that most coaches recognize the importance of teaching a good back to trust his body, to rely upon the kinesthetic sense that most backs are born with.

But several plays within any good offense invite defensive personnel to react predictably to backfield action. The counter is one such play. Early in the season we invariably find ourselves "imploring" ball carriers, especially on quick openers, to cut "against the grain," that is, to move against the rotation of the secondary in order to pick up the downfield blockers. As we all know, it works. But it doesn't work with counter plays. If anything, the ball carrier on counter plays should be encouraged to make a lateral outside move or to be prepared to "juke" the defensive halfback, who, more than any other defensive player, may represent the only obstacle between him and six points. Look at Figure 5-7.

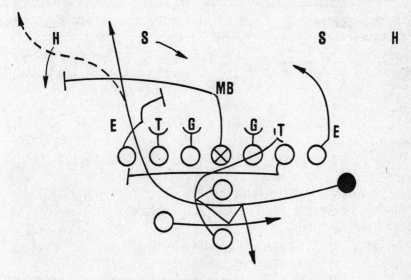

Figure 5-7

If the play is run correctly, the onside safety is likely to move to his left. The offside safety is likely to be frozen, at least momentarily. Once the wingback makes his cut behind the tackle's trap block, his best bet is to go either straight or to move quickly to his outside. The defensive halfback will be conscious of protecting the outside, so the wingback's lateral outside move downfield of the halfback is a good one, far better than cutting into a defense which has just recovered from a little embarrassment. The running of the ball is up to the ball carrier, but an occasional clue as to where the openings might be is up to the coach. That's why we make all those big bucks the school pays up. More enjoyably, having our players run for us is about the only way our squeaky knees will let us score touchdowns.

Timing

And this play will score touchdowns, especially if a few critical but easily overlooked elements of its execution are observed. Here are a few more. The timing is best if the wingback clears, in the case of the crossfire counter at 5, before the left halfback enters the line. The exact timing of the play should follow a specific sequence. After receiving the ball from the center, the quarterback gets a deep drop, faking to the fullback. As the fullback reaches the quarterback, he plants his outside foot and cuts between the pulling tackle and the wingback, who is running parallel to the line of scrimmage to receive the hand off. After faking to the fullback, the quarterback continues his full pivot, faking to the left halfback. The left halfback must execute a good fake, driving hard into the four or six hole after the wingback clears. The importance of the left halfback's fake cannot be emphasized strongly enough. His fake will help to hold the middle linebacker and to immobilize one or more players in the defensive secondary.

If the quarterback stays low during the execution of the play, it will be more successful. The element of deception will be improved. Deception also is dependent upon the timing of the fakes and the eventual hand off. We always expect the time between each of these elements to be equal. That is, one of the coaches early in the season always shouts out "Fake....Fake....Hand" when the play is being executed. If the play ends up following a "Fake....Fake........Hand" sequence, the quarterback is holding the ball too long before the handoff. Nothing makes a defensive man's job easier than seeing the quarterback holding the ball, waiting for the back to take it. The play should be exact. Just as the quarterback completes his fake to the left halfback and continues his pivot, the wingback should be almost in front of him to receive the handoff. The play involves an inside handoff, that is, the quarterback is handing the ball forward, toward the wingback who is between the quarterback and the line of scrimmage. If not timed properly, the quarterback will end up holding the ball for the defense and all the world to see. The word precision is well-chosen. And it really doesn't take that much time to make the play precise. If you explain it clearly during the first few days of practice, the kids will pick it up easily and will have the timing mastered well before the first game.

A Few Words About Line Play

The tackle should be the first lineman to master the timing. To say that the tackle is focal within the counter play is no startling revelation. Tackles are focal within most offensive plays. Their need, however, to get off the mark on counter plays and to hustle down the line of scrimmage is very important if the play is to be timed correctly. A lumbering offensive tackle who can do little more than waddle down the offensive line is the last thing a good counter play needs. For that matter, it's the last thing any offensive play needs. That kind of player might be helpful somewhere in the middle of the defensive line but not at offensive tackle. The counter play requires a big, strong athlete with moderately good speed, who can work into the line of scrimmage in order to have the proper angle on the man on the defensive line to be trapped. We have found at times that some of our best offensive tackles were converted ends, those kids who were moderately big and moderately strong but who didn't have the mobility or the pass-receiving skills of some of their smaller and more talented counterparts. If convinced early in their high school careers that they might help the team at tackle, they usually develop the mind set and the weight lifting regimen necessary to become more than serviceable offensive tackles, even excellent ones.

And they learn to *love* trap blocking. Just the mention of the term "counter play" provokes sly smiles in the huddle. Because a tackle usually finds himself involved in "hand to hand combat" with the enemy across the line, the chance to launch an "armored attack" on a defensive end comes as a welcomed diversion. In addition, it is a block which is much more visible to everyone in the stands and, as such, serves as added incentive for the tackle to make his presence "felt" by the defensive end.

A final word about the tackle involves a reconsideration of "why the tackle trap?" By way of quickly reviewing a strategy mentioned in an earlier chapter, take a look at Figure 5-8. The heavy undotted lines represent standard defensive keys. The dotted lines represent cross keys, a defensive strategy which our opponents use against us quite often, primarily because of their respect for our crossfire action. In the past we had been able to determine quite early

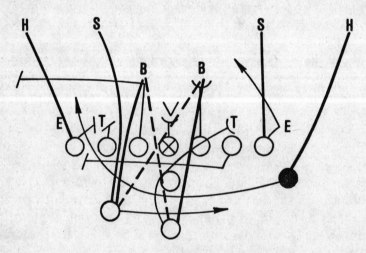

Figure 5-8

in the game which of several keys the defense was using. Lately, however, it takes us a little longer because our opponents are varying their keys based upon our formation as well as down and distance and field situation. We find with each passing year that the "cat and mouse" game gets more and more sophisticated. But that's what makes this game so much fun.

The most important consideration, however, is that regardless of which of the keys the defense uses, the counter play with the tackle trap will lead none of them to the point of attack. The linebackers are keying the backs, generally *through* the guards in order to pick up the trap action. A defensive coach probably has indicated somewhere along the line that the guards will lead the linebackers to the point of attack. The onside safety is keying the home halfback, who is leading him *away* from the point of attack. The onside defensive halfback is keying the offensive end, who *is* providing a clue regarding the point of attack. But the halfback's "outside-in" responsibility is likely to move him up and away from the wingback's eventual path. Besides, if the fullback fakes well versus the 6-1 or if either guard gets free versus the 5-2, the onside defensive halfback is going to have a very effective blocker to contend with. The only genuinely reliable key is the offside defensive halfback's, and all he can do is try his best to shout a warning to his teammates on the other side of the field. And if the offside offensive end moves straight ahead for four or five steps before he makes his move downfield, he is likely to preoccupy the defensive halfback as well as generally immobilize the offside safety.

The tackle trap, then, is one of the critical elements in the play's success. It not only gives the tackle a chance to increase his visibility; it also is one of the "sneakier" strategies you'll ever throw at a defense. It becomes, in essence, another reason why the opposing coach can't trust you. Using the counter play with a tackle trap represents one of the few times in your life when everyone's inability to trust you is an outright compliment.

A Little Bit More About Line Play

A few additional comments about strategy are needed. A good football play requires that no one take the easy way out. This is especially true of counter plays because of the momentary delay in their execution. If the play is to break down dramatically, the breakdown is likely to occur somewhere in the middle of the line. For this reason, the guards have to be especially careful to prevent penetration from the linebackers in the 5-2 or the down guards on the 6-1. Against the 5-2, the guards must be prepared to area block blitzing or scraping linebackers, and, against the 6-1, they must be careful not to cut off block or, in any way, dive at the knees of the defensive player. A cut off block may be appropriate for some plays, but the counter play is yet another of the many plays in a good offense that requires each guard to put his helmet on the numbers of the opposing player. He will not be expected to drive him back or to move him one way or the other, but he will be expected to neutralize the middle of the line. Missed assignments on either end of the offensive line may prevent a big gainer, but penetration in the middle will stop the play cold. The guards, therefore, more so than anyone else on the team, cannot take the easy way out by diving at someone's feet. We've had it happen in the past, and it will probably happen again in the future. The player who does it, though, better devise a way to protect against splinters.

Because "plateauing" of the double team block already has been mentioned in a previous chapter, there is no need to mention it again. But a few additional comments might be made about the double team block itself. First, like all double team blocks, the man head on the defensive lineman, in this case the onside tackle, is expected to "post" him, that is, to put his forehead on the numbers and prevent penetration. The offensive man to the side of the defensive lineman is responsible for "driving" him. If executed successfully, the end and tackle should be able to push the defensive tackle all the way down the line of scrimmage. Even better, they should push him at an angle away from the point of attack. In this way, the block will interfere with the onside linebacker's pursuit path, in essence "catching him in the wash."

Second, if the block is being executed against a really tough defensive tackle, the end may have to "crab block" him. In other words, if the offensive tackle posts him but the defensive tackle is still able to fight off the drive block, the end may have to drop to all fours (hence, the name "crab"), working his head and shoulder behind the tackle and driving his inside leg between the legs of the tackle. The block is particularly effective against a defensive tackle with good upper body strength. Rather than instruct the end to fight a losing battle up top, we tell him to make initial contact up top, then drop to the crab block in order to tie up the tackle's legs. And it works. We prefer, however, not to use this block because it means that the end is unable to go to the next plateau or that we cannot catch the onside linebacker in the wash. But, when needed, it *does* immobilize a good defensive tackle and allows us to do the one thing we want to do: get the running back through the hole and into the secondary.

Let's Wrap It Up

This chapter was very detailed. It had to be. The precision of an effectively executed counter play requires that every player perform his responsibility to the best of his ability and within the context of a few well-explained coaching points. It is not the kind of play that is conceived during a weekend planning session and then integrated within the offense during the following week. It should be introduced early in the season and practiced regularly before it is used in a game. Whereas precision and consistency of execution will guarantee a successful misdirection play, the lack of each will sour player and coach alike on its value. If precision is an appropriate word, so is "commitment." To develop the precision required to execute so sophisticated and successful a play, every member of the team must commit the psychic as well as the physical energy to master the assignments which will make it go.

Future chapters, especially those dealing with counter plays, will not push the precision issue to the extent that this chapter has pushed it. The point has been made; it need not be belabored any more. Implicit within everything said in subsequent chapters, however, is the continued recommendation that these plays be practiced until their execution is little more than routine. Like the student in the classroom who "overlearns" his assignments in order to master the material, each player involved in the execution of a counter play must "overlearn" *his* assignments. The repetition of the assignment need not be for extended periods of time during each practice session, but it should occur frequently, for short intervals, during each week of practice, especially early on in the season. And it need not occur to the exclusion of everything else. The repetition of fundamentals is important, too. If a coach can prepare his team in such a way, however, that each player need not think about the particulars of his assignment, he will "free up" the players to concentrate on the *determined* execution of those fundamentals. A tight practice session is warranted. Practicing the misdirection offense will be discussed in a later chapter.

6

Counters from
Our Other Series

Introduction

Every basic series used by the offense should have its counter play. The counter plays within the other series may not be as confusing to the defense or, for that matter, as successful as the crossfire counter, but their presence within the series poses a constant threat to the defense. The halfback sitting out on the wing represents much more to the defense than a blocker or a pass receiver. When tandemed with the tackle on a well-executed counter play, the wingback represents one of the offense's most successful running threats. No matter what the field situation or the backfield set, a wingback suggests the ever-present potential for misdirection and, to repeat an often-repeated point, does an awful lot to keep the defense honest.

Some backfield sets, especially under certain field situations, are more predictable than others. The Wishbone or the "full house" backfield alignments are very *un*predictable because the offense can attack either side of the offensive line with equal ease. Some teams may establish tendencies as the year progresses, "left handedness" or "right handedness" for example, but these tendencies reflect the "druthers" of the

95

team. They do not usually result from the clues provided by formations such as the Wishbone, where all the backs are "at home" most of the time. The Pro formation, on the other hand, by the very nature of the obvious strengths of the backfield alignment, provides clues as to where the offense is *likely* to run the ball. Once again to resurrect the old Green Bay Packers as an example, we know that they ran a power sweep from a Pro set formation and didn't care *who* knew it. Some teams prefer to operate this way, especially pro or college teams with "All Pro's" or "blue chippers" filling in key positions.

The high school coach operating this way, expecting year after year to overpower his opponents, is either hopelessly naive or fortunate enough to find himself in a circumstance where he is either surrounded by talent or able to recruit within a wide area. Most of us don't find ourselves in such circumstances, so we have to be more creative and less "dependable" than our opponents, especially if we choose to run out of multiple backfield sets.

Despite the recent success of the Wishbone and the Power I, most high school teams continue to incorporate a variety of backfield sets. Many may *prefer* one or two formations, but most retain the potential for, and practice their plays from, several different offensive alignments. Generally, they like the opportunities provided by a variety of backfield sets. Opposing teams, after several years of competition with each other, develop a "feel" for the opponent's strengths and weaknesses and eventually organize a well-keyed defense to stop them or, at least, to cause them a lot of frustration. The unpredictability of misdirection and the foresight to scout yourself in order to break your own tendencies are good ways to prevent an opponent from "getting your number." Retaining the opportunity to run your offense from a variety of offensive formations, however, represents another way to achieve unpredictability. Running from a double wing with motion, for example, is a good way to run away from a monster or to force the opponent into a different defense. These kinds of adjustments, however, will be discussed in a later chapter.

Our purposes at this point are to suggest a few advantages of the multiple offense and, more particularly, to discuss briefly the general characteristics of three other basic series and to diagram and explain the counter plays used within each of them. Each of the series is unique within our offensive attack. The reasons we use each one are multifold. All the reasons need not be mentioned; we will, however, mention the basic ones as well as the distinctive characteristics of each.

The Quick Series

The quick series is nothing more than the old dive series and, probably, is as old as modern day football. We call it our "quick" series because the name communicates the essence of what we want to accomplish with it. Early in the season, we explain to the kids that some plays, to be executed effectively, require momentary delays, jab steps, and the like, but the quick series, with the exception of only a few plays, requires all the speed we can muster up. We'll use it late in the game, for example, or against the type of defense that requires us "to go right at 'em." Slanting defensive fronts, scraping linebackers, or particularly quick defensive tackles who can pursue well laterally may require a "quick" dive play.

Or we might find ourselves in a circumstance where our inability to predict defensive stunts is frustrating our play-calling efforts. In other words, we may find that the defense is "guessing right" more often than we are. When our frustration becomes reflected in our team's attitude and play, a last ditch effort is to take the game to the opponent. Going right at them compromises any of the advantages they may have acquired by stunting, and it gives our players a chance to vent some of their frustrations. And we know, as does our opponent, that we still retain the potential for misdirection, through counter plays or by using slant traps or quick delays. The "quick delay," an apparent contradiction in terms, will be discussed in the next chapter.

The basics of our quick series are no different from any other team's "dive" or "drive" series. Look at Figure 6-1. The

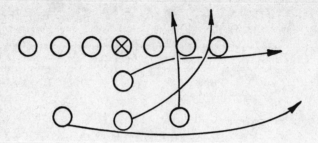

Figure 6-1

formation is a Fullhouse (Split T). Each line represents the back's path on basic plays from the series. Because we run predominantly from the Wing T, rarely will all the backs be in their "home" positions, but we prefer to introduce the series from a Fullhouse formation because it communicates to the team the basics of the series. They learn quickly, however, that the variations on this basic theme become the rule rather than the exception. The need for us to maintain the constant threat of misdirection results in our frequent use of a wingback, either from our "T" formation or the Pro. Both of these formations, as well as the Wing formation, which is used less frequently by us, can be used with the quick series. All provide the opportunity to dive both backs, as well as to option to the outside. An important point to remember as each of our series is discussed is that we can run them from just about all of our several formations. This point, although obvious to many coaches, will be discussed in a later section of this chapter, because it is so important.

A Desirable Option

Look at Figure 6-2. The formation is a Pro 8. The play is a "quick option at 8." Unlike the triple option or the Houston Veer, we do not option the fullback at four in this series. We'll do that with the inside belly. The quick option is committed to the outside. The quarterback will either keep it at a wide 6 or pitch it to the left halfback at 8. The quarterback's option is dependent upon either the decision or the pre-committed

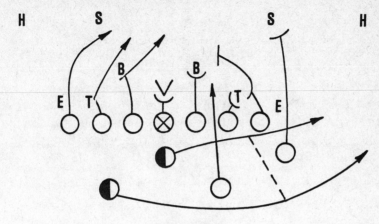

Figure 6-2

path of the defensive end. If the end stays with the pitchback, the quarterback will keep at six. If the end closes down hard, the quarterback will pitch. And if the left halfback maintains his four yard minimum distance *away* from the quarterback and his two yards in front of the quarterback, the play will get to the outside. If the left halfback stays too close to the quarterback, the defensive end will be able to cover both of them. The option element will be eliminated. Clearly, this play is similar to whatever you may be using. *Most* option plays are alike. When to call them, however, and what to complement them with are important strategies.

An Option to the Option

The option is mentioned, therefore, for two important reasons. The "Quick counter at 5" is an excellent complement to the option, especially if the backs execute well and manage to pick up some yardage to the outside. The two reasons involve the quarterback's timing and the fakes of both the quarterback and the left halfback after the ball has been handed off to the wingback. Look at Figure 6-3. The formation is the same as with Figure 6-2, a Pro 8. The play is a "Quick counter at 5" but simulates a "Quick option at 8." The quarterback's timing is critical and depends upon his ability, on the option play, to pick up the defensive end immediately and, on the counter, to find the wingback immediately. This element of execution requires the quarterback to look to the outside immediately after the snap of the ball. He should *never* look at the fullback or have to wait for him. On the counter play, he should pick up the wingback right away. He should keep him in sight as he brings the ball down the line of scrimmage, fakes to the fullback at four, and hands to the wingback.

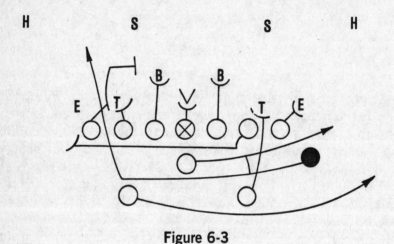

Figure 6-3

Two related points should be made. First, the quarterback's path during the execution of the play should be parallel to the line of scrimmage. On a normal dive play to the fullback at four, the quarterback moves *into* the line in order to complete the handoff as close as possible behind the offensive tackle. The fullback will then read the tackle's block and "run to daylight," anticipating any move against the grain. On the counter plays, however, the quarterback must remember to maintain a parallel path in order to avoid a collision path with the pulling tackle. He must also make a quick ball fake to the fullback, the fullback assuming the primary responsibility for executing a good fake. The quarterback and the fullback have little time to make a good mesh because the fullback's dual responsibility is to make a good fake and to fill for the pulling tackle. In most instances, especially if the defensive lineman has been instructed to follow the pulling tackle, the fullback will have to fill right off the tail of the pulling tackle, so the fake between quarterback and fullback must be executed quickly. The fake is facilitated if, like the crossfire counter, the fullback runs into the defensive tackle or gets tackled by him.

A second related point involves the handoff to the wingback. In order to avoid a fumble, the quarterback must be prepared to initiate the handoff while the wingback is still in front of him. The handoff should be *completed* by the time the wingback is alongside of him. If the handoff is *initiated* when they are side by side, the ball is likely to be placed on the wingback's hip, thereby increasing the possibility of a fumble The need to execute a good handoff is the primary reason why we instruct the quarterback to pick up the wingback immediately after he receives the snap from center. An excess of adrenalin early in the game may cause the wingback to move down the line of scrimmage a lot quicker than he normally does. When this happens, and it *will* happen sooner or later, the quarterback may have to shorten up the fake to the fullback in order to assure a good handoff to the wingback. To do this, the quarterback must have the wingback in sight throughout the entire play. Teaching the quarterback to do this normally isn't a problem, especially if the strategy is reinforced by the quarterback's similar need to keep the defensive end in sight during the execution of all the option plays.

Finishing Up the Quick Counter

During the initial part of the play, the left halfback should move parallel to the line of scrimmage, watching the quarterback and, by all appearances, anticipating a pitch from him. The quarterback, after handing the ball to the wingback, must extend his fake for a good three or four yards. His hands should be clasped in front of him, about collar high. After four or five *hard* steps to the outside, the quarterback should simulate the pitch by extending his arm *noticeably* toward the left halfback, who, in turn, should simulate catching the ball. Both the quarterback and the left halfback then should continue hard to the outside and upfield. Neither should stop after the pitch fake is executed.

Most backs tend to fake rather perfunctorily. They act as if the fake is unimportant and must be executed only to somehow complete the play. When this happens, it's our fault. During the introduction and the actual timing of the play, we emphasize faking just as much as we emphasize ball-carrying and blocking responsibilities, especially with the counter plays. The extended fakes of both backs attract the attention of the secondary, especially the safeties, who may be assigned the quarterback on option action. The longer the backs extend the fakes, the longer they will divert attention away from the point of attack on the other side of the line.

A final point to emphasize to the backs is that the "Quick counter," unlike the crossfire counter, involves an "outside" handoff, that is, the quarterback's body is positioned between the line of scrimmage and the point of exchange. Although a seemingly obvious coaching point, the wingbacks sometimes get confused regarding the point of exchange. This problem can be resolved either through constant repetition or, more effectively, by providing the opportunity early in the season for all the players, even the linemen, to see and to understand the "big picture." Their improved understanding of the play not only guarantees its refined execution but also contributes to the players' sense of involvement in the offense. Both of these by-products are well worth the time invested during a few practices early in the season.

Line Play

No mention has been made of the line play because the blocking patterns and general responsibilities are the same as for the crossfire counter. The assignments are the same for all the counter plays. For the purposes of our discussion, we have diagrammed each play versus only the 5-2 and the 6-1, because they represent the most often-used defenses by high school football teams. Because a good number of teams, however, will use variations of the 4-4, flexed defenses, monsters, or heaven knows what else, a team's practice schedules should reflect repeated opportunities to master the blocking assignments versus several defenses, especially those which have been identified as likely for an upcoming game. Ways to accommodate this in a practice schedule will be discussed in a later chapter.

The Inside Belly Series

We've been associated with the spectacle as well as the celebration of football for quite a few years now, so we can finally admit a fundamental reality: our belly is big ... the series, that is. Poor joke but valid comment, no matter which way you chose to take it originally. Our belly series, thanks to the input of Jordan Oliver and a succession of creative and knowledgeable high school coaches, has gained some excellent yardage for us and has provided loads of excitement for our fans. Unlike the Quick series, the Inside Belly series relies on deception and instructs key players to 'slow down' in order to give the defense time to react. As such, Inside Belly action requires a little finesse and a lot of acting and proves to be a minor source of frustration to the aggressive offensive player, especially early in the season.

The critical element in the series and the action around which everything else revolves is the quarterback/fullback mesh. Refer to Figure 6-4. The play is an "Inside Belly Option at 8." Like the triple option, the quarterback's mesh with the fullback involves only two steps. His first step is at a 45 degree angle away from the center and toward the fullback: his second is another 45 degree angle, with the fullback, toward the line of scrimmage. That's it; no more, no less. As any coach who runs either the triple option or any belly series knows, it ain't as easy as it sounds.

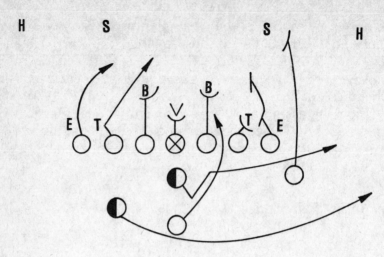

Figure 6-4

The mesh between quarterback and fullback requires hours of practice if the ride into the line of scrimmage is to influence the defense long enough to set up the outside plays. Quarterback and fullback each have to be confident that one will be where the other expects him to be. This comment is especially true when the play is an option at seven or eight, because, like the quick option, we require the quarterback to find the defensive end immediately. He has no time, therefore, to look for the fullback first. This is a very important point. Defensive ends are not on our payroll, they are not required to act predictably, nor are they required to respect our reputation or the physical well-being of our quarterback.

If the quarterback hurries the ride or concentrates on the fullback during the ride, a hard-charging defensive end will bury him. If only from a sense of self-preservation, the quarterback must realize the importance of finding the defensive end and of adjusting his own actions based upon what he does. If he boxes or, in any way, faces up with backfield action to play a waiting game, the quarterback must challenge him, in essence force him to make a choice between himself or the pitchback. If he comes hard, normally on a pre-committed path to the inside, the quarterback may have to pitch the ball to the halfback as soon as he removes it from the fullback's "belly." This is the primary reason why the halfbacks are instructed to anticipate an immediate pitch. If, on those welcomed occasions, the defensive end's mental lapse results in his going for the fullback's fake (and it'll happen, more often than you'd think), the quarterback should move quickly around the end and be prepared to option the next man to show, probably the defensive halfback. It is also a good idea to inform the refs before the game of the inside belly play, especially if its execution results in a swarm of defensive players around the fullback. More often than just a few times we have heard the ref's whistle while our quarterback was racing downfield for an apparent touchdown. A good fullback who can drop his shoulder and bow into the middle of the line just as the quarterback removes the ball from his pocket can attract a lot of attention from the defense and provoke an inadvertent whistle from the ref.

Because during the option play the fullback is instructed to hit a "wide 2 hole" at about three-quarter speed, the quarterback's need to watch the defensive end is especially critical. The slower ride attracts more attention from the defense and gives them added time to react to the fullback, but it also allows more time for the defensive end to penetrate. So after the ride a quick pitch is often warranted.

Use a Little Finesse, Too

The finesse block, mentioned in an earlier chapter, is a great strategy when the fullback is running the ball at the three and four holes. Look at Figure 6-5. Neither the defensive tackle nor the defensive end is blocked. As indicated earlier, such a blocking strategy keeps the defense guessing and can cause considerable confusion, especially if combined with the several other complementary blocking strategies which have been described earlier. Two additional advantages remain.

One, the movements of the defensive players are easily observed if no one is blocking them. If the defensive end, for example, wants to react to the fullback on the inside belly at

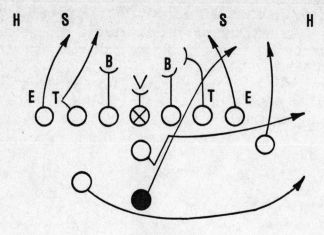

Figure 6-5

four, he can be observed doing so immediately, at which point the inside belly option at eight is a natural, which fact suggests the second advantage. The inside belly *option* can involve the same blocking scheme, which results in a lot of trouble for the middle linebacker as well as the onside safety. The "sameness" of the play is one of the big advantages of the entire series.

A third play also is very similar. The inside belly at five or six uses the same blocking scheme but puts the defensive end in a no-win situation. Look at Figure 6-6. The play is designed to beat the defensive end and the onside defensive halfback who chase hard to the outside to neutralize the pitch threat. Their pursuit to the outside opens up the off-tackle hole. If the defensive tackle goes for the fullback's fake and if the offensive end and wingback eliminate the onside safety, the left halfback has only to run straight into the end zone. The series as described thus far is very much like the triple option. The backfield paths and execution are much the same; the line blocking is similar; and the defensive clues to watch for are alike.

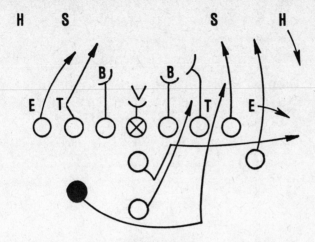

Figure 6-6

Our intent never was to incorporate the triple option into our offensive attack. We may have modified our blocking schemes somewhat as we observed the successes of some wishbone/triple option teams, but the inside belly always has been an important series within our offense, as a matter of fact, long before the triple option came on the scene. It is more coincidental than anything else that the inside belly looks so much like the triple option.

The Inside Belly Counter

A significant variation from the tendencies of most triple option teams and an important part of our inside belly series, the counter play is a perfect complement to the inside belly plays at four, six, and option at eight. Like the counter plays described earlier, it simulates the backfield action of the basic series, is quick-hitting, and is easily executed. Look at Figures 6-7 and 6-8. Figure 6-7 diagrams the counter at five, Figure 6-8 the counter at three vs. the 5-2.

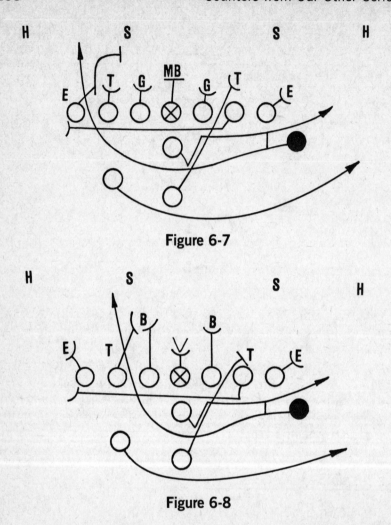

Figure 6-7

Figure 6-8

Perhaps the most notable characteristic of the inside belly counter is that it is similar in appearance to the quick counter. The line blocking is the same for all the counter plays; the fullback always fills for the pulling tackle; and the timing, especially between the quarterback and the wing-back, has to be precise. The inside belly counter, again like the quick counter, involves an outside hand off, the quarter-back's body being between the line of scrimmage and the point of exchange.

The quarterback again has the responsibility of meshing with the fullback, riding him into the four hole, keeping his eye on the wingback the entire time, executing a safe exchange with the wingback, and continuing his fake well to the outside of the right offensive end's original position. The ride with the fullback must not be hurried, a fact which is true of most of the inside belly plays. A quick ride to the fullback on the option play hurries the quarterback to his own funeral; on the counter play the same is true of the wingback. The attention of the defense has to be drawn to the fullback, and later to the quarterback as he continues his fake with the left halfback to the outside.

The hand off to the wingback, therefore, must be quick but fluid. It must be exchanged carefully and confidently, but it must not disrupt the basic flow of the play. In other words, the actual exchange of the ball between quarterback and wingback must happen so quickly that the attention of the defense remains focused on either the fullback or the option possibilities to the outside.

The speed of the fullback into the line will be influenced somewhat by his quickness as well as by the quickness of the pulling tackle. For purposes of timing and the effective execution of the play, the assumption must be that the defensive tackle will follow the offensive tackle, or at least become inside conscious when the tackle pulls. The fullback, therefore, must fill right off the tail of the pulling tackle, being prepared for immediate contact. If he arrives late and fails to fill the hole, the defensive tackle's penetration can stop the play cold.

The fullback's assignment in filling for the tackle is the same as with the other counter plays. If he drops his shoulder after the fake and prevents the tackle's penetration by running into him, the fullback not only will help to seal the middle of the line but also will execute a better fake. This play tends to be one of our most effective counter plays. It has everything a good counter play must have. It hits quickly, and the backfield action of the basic series is diversified enough to hold the attention of the defense.

Of most importance, however, the basic plays within the inside belly series are very successful for us, the option especially. It represents one of the few consistently effective ways for us to get to the outside during those years when we don't have exceptional speed in the backfield. If you'll take a close look at the inside belly at 6 again (Figure 6-6), you'll see that it, too, is effective in getting the offense to the outside.

Getting a play around the end does not require blazing backfield speed. It involves a careful analysis of defensive stunts and tendencies followed by the right call. We have seen several inexperienced freshman coaches with excellent backfield speed find themselves unable to "turn the corner." You've seen it, too: at the snap of the ball twenty-two players run for the sidelines, the ball carrier leading the way— barely.

The inside belly at six, complemented by the inside belly option at eight, can do much to relieve such a problem, if the coach is watching the defense carefully and if he sequences properly. In addition, if he uses the counter play at the right time, he not only may pick up big yardage if the defense over-rotates, but also will reaffirm the strength of the basic plays within the inside belly series.

The Power Series

The term "power" is used in our football vocabulary much the same way as we use the term "quick." It is descriptive of what we want the kids to do and of how we want them to think. Whereas "quick" communicates "speed," "power" communicates "tough" and "force." Look at Figure 6-9. This play doesn't involve any razzle dazzle, as everyone knows. It takes the action to the opponent and challenges him to stop the play.

It may involve *some* strategy. We have observed on several different occasions, for example, that some defensive lines slant into the long side of the field, regardless of our backfield set. When this happens, we run a power right from a Pro set *into* the short side of the field. It won a conference

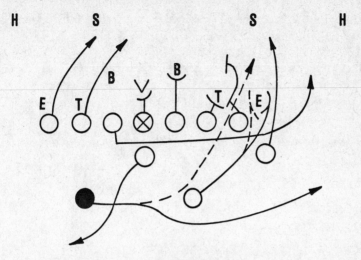

Figure 6-9

championship for us once, not just because we executed well but because we had scouted ourselves and had determined before the game that we *had* been running most of our wide plays into the long side of the field. Because our opponent had made the same determination, we broke all our tendencies for the championship game and thoroughly confused his defensive keys.

But normally the power right or the power left is a "Here we come" kind of play. Certainly we have complements to the power right, which serve to keep defenses honest, but the primary play within the series is the end run. We *can* run slant traps (to be discussed in the next chapter), reverses, traps, and the ever-threatening counter, but the power right or left remains the most frequently run play in the series.

A Little About the Line

The line blocking is self-explanatory. We always pull the "guard off" and lead with the fullback. The "guard on" always blocks the man directly in front of him. Against the 6-1 or any even-man front, no "right-minded" coach would pull the onside guard anyway. We don't pull him versus the 5-2 either, because we would rather not provide an obvious key to the onside linebacker, a player who is likely to be one of the best tacklers on the opposing team. If we can immobilize the onside linebacker for just a split second by not pulling the guard, we might catch him in the wash if the double team block is executed well, or the onside end might be able to cut him down if the end is able to plateau to the next level.

One coaching point for the pulling guard is very important. The point has application for other plays as well, particularly those which require the guard just to lead the play and to have no specific assignment. Once the guard turns the corner to lead the play upfield, he *must* look to the inside *immediately* to cut off any pressure coming from the safeties, linebacker(s), or defensive linemen. Most power plays break down because a linebacker or an aggressive, well-reacting safety sneaks in behind the lead blockers and trips up the ball carrier. Such a play is not only bothersome to the coaches on the sidelines but also demoralizing to the team on the field. Nothing is more frustrating to a player or coach than to see well-executed blocks downfield and a tripped up ball carrier somewhere near the line of scrimmage. If the leading guard is "inside conscious" as he paves the way for the ball carrier, he likely will make a key block and get a few "oooo's" and "ahhh's" from the crowd.

Be in the Right Play at the Right Time

While coming down the line of scrimmage, the guard must also be aware of the fullback's block on the defensive end. If the end is boxing and facing up with backfield action, the fullback is instructed to blow him out in order to open up the six hole for the left halfback. If the end is slashing in order to stack up the action in the backfield, the fullback is instructed to cut him down, in which case the left halfback will run wide. The guard must read these blocks if he is to lead the ball carrier to the right hole.

We found that the play is much more effective when we give the fullback the option of how to block the defensive end. Formerly, we called the play either a "Power at 6" or a "Power at 8." We found, however, that the unpredictability of defensive stunts, especially line stunts, often caused us to be in the right play at the wrong time. Giving the fullback the responsibility to decide on the best block to use enabled us to counteract the defensive stunts. Although it required that the guard and the running back be especially aware of the fullback's block, it assured us that we would be in the right play at the *right* time, and it encouraged our players to be involved and to acknowledge the importance of teamwork.

We have several other plays within the power series. The power right and the power left, however, are the primary plays within the series and provide the proper backfield action for the counter play.

The Power Counter

When the team starts picking up yardage to the outside, and the defense, especially the secondary, starts rotating on the action of the offensive backfield, the counter play is a good call for two reasons. One, it is a good ground gainer in its own right. Two, by making the defense conscious of misdirection, it keeps them honest when the power right is called again. Look at Figures 6-10 and 6-11. The formation is a Pro 8. The play is a "Power counter at 5" versus the 5-2 and the 6-1. As described in an earlier chapter, the backfield action will encourage the secondary to rotate away from the intended point of attack, especially the onside safety, who probably is keying the home halfback.

The line blocking is the same as the other counter plays, and the backfield action is quite simple. Although the fullback again is filling for the pulling tackle, his angle is fundamentally the same as the angle he takes for the defensive end on the power right, so it provides no clues to the defense.

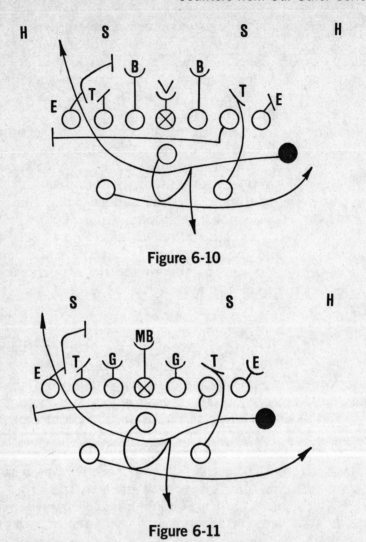

Figure 6-10

Figure 6-11

The one clue that a poorly executed power counter *can* provide for the defense is the ball in the hands of the quarterback for too long a period of time. Because the power counter is the one counter play which involves only one fake while the quarterback simultaneously is getting depth in the backfield, he is easily observed by the defense if the play isn't timed correctly. For that reason, we instruct the left halfback to cheat "up and in" on one step, in order to get a better mesh with the quarterback. The quarterback is instructed to make a very pronounced fake to the left halfback, even to ride him for a step or two, before he pivots to make the hand off to the wingback. By extending the fake a step or two longer, he will be concealing the ball from the defense better, and he will be making his pivot wide enough to make the exchange behind the *offside* offensive guard. Remember, the exchange at that point is needed if the back is to get the ball soon enough to get control of it and to make a good, controlled cut into the five hole. Look at Figures 6-10 and 6-11 again. The diagrammed path of the quarterback illustrates the point.

Finally, after the handoff, the quarterback drops back hard to simulate a play action pass. His execution of this final fake is very important if he is to have any influence on the defensive secondary. We even have had quarterbacks who were sharp enough to fake throwing a pass, a gesture which, on occasion, attracted just enough defensive attention to cause them to pause momentarily in their search for the ball. Such a move from the quarterback is carrying "faking" to the "nth" degree, but that may be just what a play needs to go all the way. Encourage it: it has great carry-over value for player involvement, too.

Complement the Good Stuff

Like most good offensive attacks, all the series mentioned in this chapter, along with the crossfire series, complement each other in the sense that each can be run from just about any formation. The T 8 formation, for example, can result in a quick at 3, an inside belly at 6, a crossfire trap at 4, a crossfire at 1, or an inside belly counter at 5. Obviously, many other plays are possible, as are many other formations. The important point is that we can hit any hole along the line of scrimmage from just about any formation.

Even though we think we're pretty special, even we have to admit that our offense is not unique in this regard. What we *do* keep in mind, however, and what many other teams can lose sight of so easily, is the need to increase our unpredictability not only by using misdirection but by scouting ourselves to avoid a predictable pattern of play calling. Some predictability is unavoidable because the "special mix" of our personnel makes us better at running some plays than others. We don't worry about that kind of predictability. A little bit of the "Here we come and we don't care who knows it" philosophy is fine.

But it had better be bolstered by good execution and sound fundamentals if it is to work. And it better not be the exclusive thrust of your game plan. Most importantly, it should not result from that insidious tendency that plagues all of us, that habit of calling favorite plays from favorite formations, of sliding predictability into another series or into a sequenced play if our original game plan doesn't seem to be working. It happens at one time or another to all of us, and, worst of all, we usually don't realize it. So scout yourself and sustain the complementary relationship of your offense, especially once you make counter plays an integrated part of your ground attack.

Let's Wrap It Up

We like the counter plays—all of them. They have done a lot for our offense. They are fun to run and fun to teach, and they work. One point that seems to require early mention and frequent reminder during the first few days involves the point of exchange. During and several times *after* the intro-duction of each play, remind the backs, the quarterbacks and the halfbacks especially, that the "quick" and "inside belly" counters involve the *outside* handoff, and the "power" and "crossfire" counters involve the *inside* handoff. If you fail to drill this into them early in the season, they'll plague you with the same question throughout half the year. If they pick it up early, they will execute more confidently, and you'll maintain your sanity a little longer—at least in relationship to teaching counter plays. They may get you somewhere else, but you'll be proud of the counters!

Finally, if the defense starts chasing the pulling tackle and if your fullback, no matter how hard he tries, just can't block the chasing lineman, "influence pull" the tackle once or twice and run the fullback where the defensive lineman *was*. Such a tactic will keep the defense honest, and the fullback will enjoy running right by an unblocked and somewhat embarrassed defensive lineman. It probably will become a big gainer in its own right.

The great advantage of counter plays, as with some other forms of misdirection, is their ability to integrate with almost any offensive system. Any team that runs or *can* run out of a winged formation can use the counter play. It complements any basic series. Its most distinctive characteristic, especially as we use it, is the tackle trap. The tackle trap is the single most obvious reason for the success of the play. Of several teams that might use the counter play, all else being equal—knowledge of strategy, proper execution, similar personnel—the team that uses the tackle trap will be the most successful with the counter. And almost any tackle can trap—and enjoy it. You, too, will enjoy it when you experience what it can do for your ground game and for the revitalization of your whole system.

7

Slant Traps and
Quick Delays:
The Fast and the
Slow of Misdirection

Let's Start with the Slant Trap

Every play within the crossfire series contains misdirection, and most of them are quite easy to execute. Considering the types of plays involved and the basic simplicity of their design, the plays within the crossfire series provide the easiest way to execute misdirection. Slant traps are probably the next easiest. They are quick hitting, easy to execute, involve easily learned blocking schemes, and, like most misdirection plays, serve as excellent complements to the plays within the basic series. The characteristic that distinguishes them from most other elements of misdirection is the speed with which they hit the point of attack. The quick slant trap, for example, hits the point of attack faster than almost any other play within the quick series.

The same probably is true of the power slant trap, which hits the hole just about as fast as the power trap at four. An advantage most of the time, the quickness of the slant trap can be a disadvantage for the fullback who is unable to run to daylight or who gets easily tripped up by an arm tackle. The nature of our offense, however, and the use we make of our fullback demand that we have a strong runner, with good balance and good kinesthetic sense. We have been fortunate to have such players at the fullback position.

The slant traps have no special significance for the line. They simply involve another trap play for the guards. Although we would like all our linemen to understand the "big picture," and certainly we make the annual attempt, their understanding of the *basic* blocking is critical, so we keep it simple. Considering the variety of defenses the linemen may expect to see during the course of one season, the simplicity of the blocking schemes is additionally important.

The "big picture" is not nearly as important for the line as it is for the backs. The linemen depend on the backs to pick up yardage and, ultimately, to score points; the backs depend on the line for their physical well-being! If the back forgets to favor the double-team block on the noseman and to *see* the guard's trap block, he may never find the hole or may even run outside the trap block and get tackled on the line of scrimmage and, later, on the sidelines by half the coaching staff. Timing practice for the backs, therefore, must involve line blocking, even if the third or fourth team line must block dummies for them or just run through their assignments while the backs run the plays.

Another Word for Precision

Slant traps, as much as any other misdirection play, involve split-second timing. Look at Figure 7-1. The play is a power slant trap at 1 versus the 5-2. The backfield execution is limited to a small area, generally from tackle to tackle, so the hand off is made within a split second of the snap from center. After the hand off, the ball carrier must run through some traffic at the point of attack and make a good cut, generally to the outside if the rest of the backs execute their fakes well.

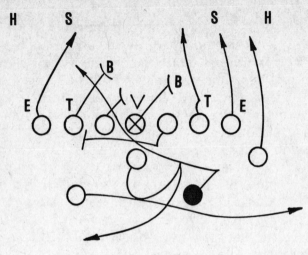

Figure 7-1

The slant traps are simple in design and are relatively easy to learn, but they rely on several fine points of execution if they are to be successful. These points will be discussed in later sections of this chapter.

When Is the Right Time?

There are several "right times" to use slant traps, all of which depend on a well-coordinated sideline staff looking for clues during play and an involved offensive team gaining knowledge of the opponent during each possession of the ball. Also, the "right time" for the slant trap and its eventual success depends in large part on the earlier success of its complement. The "power right," for example, should be run several times to condition the defense to think "power to the outside" when they see the Pro 8 formation. The primary plays within the power and even the quick series often are run out of the Pro 8 formation and usually involve little more than straight ahead stuff. They encourage defenses to pursue on backfield action, especially if the plays being run are successful. So conditioned, the defense is susceptible to the slant trap.

An observation already mentioned several times but worth repeating several times more, the element of misdirection on an offensive attack not only will gain yardage in its own right but also will reestablish the effectiveness of the plays it complements. If the "power right," for example, is suddenly being stopped by the defense, they must be rushing troops to the outside to stop it. The slant trap will hit the defense where those troops probably *were*. Because it is likely to pick up at least *some* yardage, it will thicken the plot for the defense. Their sudden consciousness of the slant trap will provoke a little hesitation in them the next time they see the Pro 8 formation. The success of the power right is thus reestablished.

"Oh, dear lord of befuddled football coaches, if only it were that easy!" "When put down on paper, it all seems to fall into place, but on game days nothing is simple." The point made in this chapter, however, is that it *can* be that simple. If the offense is well-coordinated and determines the strengths and the weaknesses of the defense, and does so systematically, the actual calling of plays is quite easy. It is particularly easy if the offensive coach has a variety of plays to choose from, the sequencing of which (a key point) can hit any hole along the line of scrimmage from any formation. Every basic series sequences, but usually to the same side of the line of scrimmage. Not true with misdirection. Look at Figure 7-1 again. The play simulates action to the offensive backfield's right but actually hits the one, maybe even the three, hole versus the 5-2. Misdirection enables a team to hit any spot on the line of scrimmage, thereby establishing their unpredictability and keeping them ahead of the defense, even in a guessing game.

You can win even the guessing game if you chart the defense and catch them in a predictable pattern of stunts. The least you can do is determine the "why" of their stunts, even if the pattern is not predictable. The "why" probably involves their compensation for some weakness in the defense. This assumption is not always true, because many defenses use stunts just to keep the offense off guard. In many instances, however, the defense is covering up *something*. On that basis, set up some hypotheses and hit 'em hard. One of them is likely to work.

Assume, for example, that a weakness is the defensive team's slow pursuit to the outside, so they slant the defensive line to the wide side of the field, not all the time nor in any predictable pattern, but clearly more than to the short side of the field. You might try several things, two of which are mentioned here.

You can reinforce their thinking by running a couple of power plays to the wide side and letting them stop you or, at least, hold you down to minimal gains, then run the counter back to the short side. More appropriately and strategically smarter, you can hit their perceived weakness by running the powers to the short side of the field and, when they adjust, you can run the power counter back to the wide side.

Next, assume that the defense has two tough line-backers, not good readers, but fast and aggressive tacklers. So the opposing coach scrapes them a lot, generally into the wingback. Look at Figure 7-2. Aside from any of several passes which might be used, the power slant trap is a

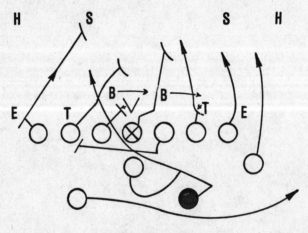

Figure 7-2

natural. The blocking scheme involves a double team block on the noseman, the guard having the option to "plateau" to the next man, usually the offside linebacker. On this play, however, the noseman is coming, so the guard has to take him. The onside tackle, normally responsible for the onside linebacker, because the linebacker is running away from him, can plateau to the next level, the offside safety. The left end's block on the onside safety, his normal assignment, completes the play and sets up a good gainer.

All these strategies, as well as others mentioned thus far, rely upon smart observation on the sidelines. Slant traps provide such good ammunition that most coaches quickly develop the strategic know-how to determine when to use them.

What About the Quick Delays?

The same is true of them. They also are fun to call. An apparent contradiction in terms, the quick delay is a part of the quick series but involves a momentary delay for the ball carrier, hence its name. Look at Figure 7-3. The play is a "Quick delay at 1." The formation is a T 8. The quick delay is particularly effective for us out of the T 8 because we run most of our crossfire action from the T wing. We also run some fullback quicks at 2. When we *do* run the fullback quick at 2, it looks an awful lot like our inside belly action, but on those occasions when we need a hard and fast entry into the 2 hole, the "fullback quick at 2" is a good play. In addition, it is consistent with our terminology. And if the quick delay at 1 just happens to look like a backfield counter play off the inside belly action, so much the better!

When we line up in a T 8, many of our opponents instruct their linebackers in a 5-2 to cross key us. That is, the left linebacker (defensively) is responsible for our left half-back; the right linebacker for the fullback. Again, their reasoning involves the success of our crossfire series. Cross keying they think, helps them compensate for our element of misdirection.

If we observe cross keying by the defense, we use the quick delay, as well as many other plays within the quick series. The fullback's entry into the two hole influences the right linebacker to move one or two steps to his left. The fullback's entry also influences the left linebacker, who is likely to believe that the play is coming at *him* because of the

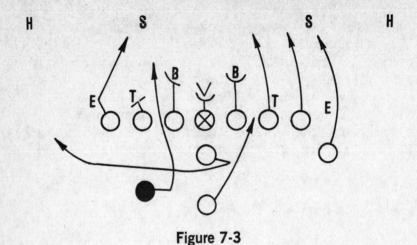

Figure 7-3

right guard's block. The initial movement of the backfield influences the defense just enough to set up the left guard's block on the onside linebacker. So a "delayed quick" becomes a pretty good play.

The Nuts and Bolts of Each

Precision and smart execution are both very important elements in the success of each play. Look at Figure 7-4. The play is a "Power slant trap at 2" versus the 6-1. The formation is a Pro 7. The line blocking is no different from the short trap blocking within many of the other plays within our offense. Nothing much need be said about it other than some brief mention of the right guard's blocking technique. The guards must learn early in the season, especially if the man over them is to be trapped, to make shoulder contact with him before going to their primary assignment, in this case, the middle linebacker. Because the defense is responsible for keeping the offensive line *off* the linebackers, they are told to make contact with the man in front of them. But the defensive lineman also knows that if he is to make the tackle, he must be free of all blockers. The old maxim, "React to pressure," applies.

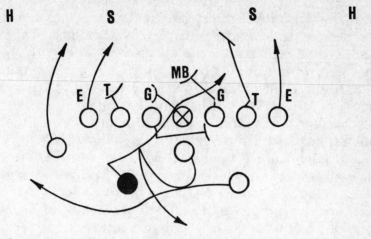

Figure 7-4

So if the offensive guard makes contact with the defensive guard, the defender probably will try to *get rid* of him, which will do two things. One, it will free up the offensive guard to block the middle linebacker. Two, it will set up the defensive man for the left guard's trap block.

The Backs Have More to Remember

Again, precision and smart execution are important. Refer once again to Figure 7-4. Several elements of this play are essential if it is to be run effectively. The most important element involves the fullback. On the regular power left, the fullback has the responsibility of blocking the right defensive end. The right halfback reads his block and cuts either to the outside or directly up field. The timing of the slant trap requires that the fullback take one step toward the defensive right end, plant his left foot, and angle back to the two hole behind the left guard's trap block. While he is taking his lead step with his left foot, although his body is pointed toward the defensive end, his *eyes* are watching the left guard. Some fullbacks make the mistake of moving toward the end and looking at him. When they make the cut to slant into the two hole, they often are unable to find the trapping guard.

They also must remember to stay low in order to lose themselves in the backfield action and behind the offensive line. The same is true of the quarterback during the initial few steps of execution. He must stay low while pivoting to fake to the right halfback. When he reaches the right half-back, he must ride him, much like a belly fake, until he pivots almost full circle, at which point he hands the ball quickly to the fullback and turns to complete his bootleg fake at eight, much the same way he would fake after the regular power play. This bootleg maneuver, by the way, will be mentioned in a later chapter when we discuss passing.

After he completes the handoff to the fullback, an *inside* handoff (the fullback will be between the quarterback and the line of scrimmage), he should show himself while running hard to the outside, his hand on his right hip as if concealing the ball. Few quarterbacks ever really appreciate the importance of this fake, unless they draw the end toward them or have a chance to observe the secondary while watching films after the game. A good bootleg fake will catch the attention of the safety and certainly the defensive half-back, who has the responsibility of stopping or at least containing outside action. If the quarterback attracts their attention at the right time, they may miss the fullback, who should be right on top of them.

A final point to remember involves the right halfback, who is faking the power left. He should remember to cheat *up* and *in* one step in order to help the quarterback with the fake. If he stays too deep, the quarterback will never get to him, or, if he does, will never get back to make the hand off to the fullback. After the quarterback completes the fake, the halfback must run hard to the outside, his body positioned as if carrying the ball. He, too, must realize the importance of his influence on the defensive secondary. Too few backs recognize this as a critical part of the play. They must learn that a good fake is often better than a good block. It may not get as good a crowd reaction, but it sure keeps the coaches smiling.

The Quick Slant Trap

The quick slant trap involves the same blocking scheme for the line. It need not be discussed again. Look at Figure 7-5. This play is quite simple and is very effective against an aggressive middle linebacker, who reacts immediately to the quarterback's opening few steps. At the snap of the ball, the quarterback moves parallel to the line of scrimmage, as if to hand to the fullback at four. The fullback takes one step forward with his right foot (keeping the pulling guard in sight), plants his right foot, and cuts diagonally into the one hole behind the guard's trap block. The quarterback makes the *outside* hand off (his own body is between the fullback and the line of scrimmage) and continues parallel to the line of scrimmage as if to option the defensive end.

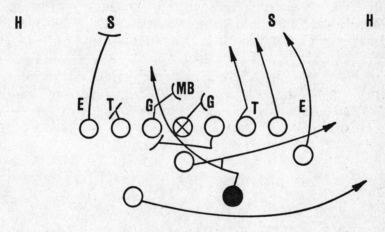

Figure 7-5

Again, the continuation of the backfield movement *after* the hand off is critical if the play is to pick up yardage. The option fakes executed by the quarterback and the left half-back will attract the attention of the secondary and, if the secondary is rotating on backfield action, will draw them out of position to react to the fullback.

An element which contributes to the success of the quick slant trap is the shielded hand off. Because the quarterback's body is between the fullback and the line of scrimmage, the hand off is difficult to see, and the element of deception is improved.

The Quick Delay: Some Specifics

The quick delay is somewhat different from the misdirection plays described thus far. Like the counter dive in the standard triple option offense, the misdirection involves the *quarterback's* change of direction and the *suggestion*, initially at least, that the backfield action is moving uniformly to the right or to the left, depending upon the play. Look at Figure 7-6. The play is a "Quick delay at 2" versus the 6-1. The formation is a T 7. As mentioned earlier, the fake to the fullback is similar to inside belly action. The primary difference is that the fullback is hitting the one hole, and there is no ride involved in the play. Because we often run "the fullback quick at 1 or 2," especially if the linebackers are cross keying, the delay action is not confusing to our players, and the terminology is consistent with our basic offense.

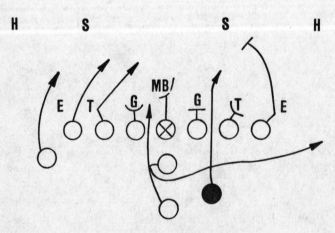

Figure 7-6

Two Ways from Each Formation

We also can run a "Quick delay at 1" from the same formation. This time the fullback, the player nearest to the hole, gets the ball. Look at Figure 7-7. The formation still is a T 7. This variation of the quick delay has been very successful for us, more so than the delay with the halfback carrying the ball. The difference results not from the running skills of the respective backs but from the basic execution of the play.

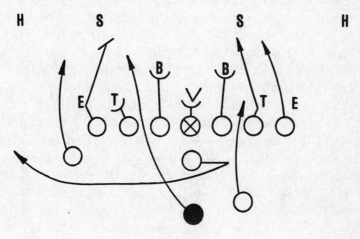

Figure 7-7

The "Quick delay at 1" from the T 7 involves a better concealed hand off and a more deceptive play, especially if it is executed quickly and if the quarterback fakes hard to the outside after the hand off. If the fullback stays low while taking his initial step toward the six hole, he is hardly noticeable until he breaks into the secondary.

The "Quick delay," then, can be run two different ways from each formation. The Pro formation involves a few minor adjustments in order to enable the quarterback to execute a good fake before making the hand off. You can make such adjustments as you decide to integrate any or all of these plays into your ground game. Which of the two home backs gets the ball should not be confusing for the players. The one who is nearest to the point of attack gets the ball.

Help Them See the Daylight

As mentioned in a previous chapter, we refrain as much as possible from telling our backs where to run on each play. At times we'll provide some clues, but the actual running to daylight is up to the ball carrier. As a matter of fact, early in the season when we discuss and practice running technique, one basic principle of running is emphasized over all others. The backs are told to think about the unique character of the play being called and, while approaching the line of scrim-mage, to look at the defensive set for any obvious blocking angles for the linemen at the point of attack. Then, at the snap of the ball, they are instructed to *stop thinking* and to let their bodies do the rest of the work. They have to let their *bodies* do the thinking. Any other kind of thought process, because of the time required to translate thought into action, can be momentarily immobilizing and can result in medi-ocre running.

The quick delay, however, is one of the few exceptions to this rule. We don't really tell the backs exactly where to run on the quick delay, but we do tell them, especially the halfbacks, to be conscious of a cut to the outside. The onside linebacker in the 5-2 defense is likely to move a step or two toward the fullback's fake, thereby setting up the guard's block. A cut to the outside is likely for the halfback. Look again at Figure 7-3 to see what we mean.

This exception to the basic rule does not obviate the rule. It merely provides a clue for the ball carrier on this play. Thinking with one's body still is critical for a good runner. He must *feel* the play and the movement of his body while he runs. As any good basketball player knows, a good shooter doesn't *think* the ball through the hoop; he *feels* it through the hoop. So it is with a good runner. He *feels* the hole and the movement to daylight; he cannot *think* it. But we can provide an occasional clue as to where it might be. We have to get our kicks, too.

Let's Wrap It Up

As far as misdirection goes, slant traps and quick delays are quite easy to execute. The simplicity of their design may cause some coaches to overlook them while searching for needed offensive adjustments. Many of us make the mistake of thinking that something must be complicated to be good. The essence of football, like the essence of anything creative, is simplicity. The need for sophistication can be satisfied by the *processes* we develop for determining strategy. *That*, at times, can become complicated. Even that, however, is most effective when kept simple.

So use the slant traps and the quick delay; just be sure to use them at the right times. Even the simplest play consistently will win football games if it is executed precisely, enthusiastically, and *opportunely*. Our job, then, as good football coaches, is to analyze the opponent's defense. We spend much of our time early in the season determining and practicing what we do well. Obviously, some of what we do well will change each year, based upon the changing talents of our personnel and the individual growth of our coaching staff. But we do not make many changes each year; the offense we have developed is pretty adaptable to differences in personnel.

The important point is that we determine our strengths, our offensive pluses, and then practice them until they've been refined and are executed confidently by every key player. We will continue to be open to change throughout the remainder of the year, for the chemical mix of our offense may change as new players earn starting positions or as scouting reports may require new strategies. Once we are into the season, however, we do not place the same emphasis upon what *we* do well. We begin to emphasize the identification of what the opponent does poorly.

The development of processes which enable us to make such determinations *before* and *during* a game gives us the knowledge and the assurance that goes with it to call a slant trap at the right time. And the misdirection they provide gives us all the other advantages mentioned earlier.

Slant traps are also very effective as the basis for play-action passes. The backfield movement is restricted to a small area; the ball is concealed well; and the play action takes just long enough to "free up" the receivers. These pass plays, along with several other play-action passes, will be discussed in Chapter 9.

8

Misdirection and
Play-Action Passing

Passing in Review

We have scouted hundreds of football games within the past several years and have observed that many, maybe most, coaches pass the ball when just about everyone in the stands and on the field *expects* them to pass the ball. Passing may be regarded by many coaches as a "catch up" strategy. Because "catch up" is for hot dogs, the smart football coach is going to coordinate his running and passing plays into a unified and well-integrated offensive attack. He is *not* going to be like the coach who regards passing and running as necessary but generally unrelated characteristics of offensive football.

The coach who recognizes the complementary relationship between misdirection and his basic series will recognize a similar relationship between running and play-action passing. A well executed play-action pass initially will resemble a running play and will put a lot of pressure on the defensive secondary. If the receivers have good technique and if the backfield executes convincing fakes, the secondary will never be able to predict throughout the entire game if the offense is running or passing. Once they become uncertain

133

about their offensive keys, they play much of the game flat-footed.

And a flat-footed safety is good to no one but the offense. His uncertainty represents one of the great advantages of play-action passing. It helps to establish not only the passing game but the running game as well. Most safeties are instructed to key either the wingback or the end and the offensive tackle. The tackle's actions are excellent predictors of what the offense is doing. If the end, for example, releases downfield, the safety may not be immediately certain if the play is a pass or a run. So the tackle's actions become important. If he releases downfield, too, the play definitely is a run, probably to the other side of the line of scrimmage. If he pass blocks, the safety can get some depth in his area to anticipate a pass. But if the wingback releases toward the safety as if to block him and if the tackle "fires out" at the man directly in front of him, the safety is likely to think RUN, especially if he has been stalked earlier in the game. At this point, the safety is in trouble, especially if the pass receivers execute good technique. Of the techniques and strategies available to them, "stalking" is the most important.

"Stalking," as illustrated in Figure 8-1, is an effective downfield blocking technique and the perfect complement to play-action passing. Safeties are aggressive football players. They like to hit people. So the most effective way to block them is to let them make the first move. On the power right, for example, the wingback is instructed to cut down the safety. He is taught to move aggressively toward the safety, to stalk him, then to cut him down when the safety commits to an inside (notice the dotted line) or an outside pursuit path.

"Stalking" a defender before blocking him is an excellent blocking technique. It keeps the blocker faced up with the man to be blocked, and it enables the blocker to maintain good control of his body. Good stalking technique requires that the wingback assume a good blocking position, move toward the defender at half to three-quarter speed, stay

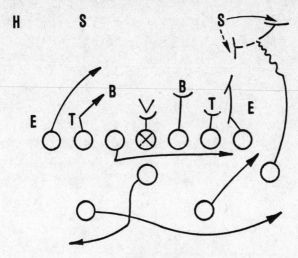

Figure 8-1

faced up with him, and drive *through* the defender's knees when the defender commits to a pursuit path. It works well. It has eliminated the costly "air blocks" that many of our downfield blockers used to make.

Stalking also is the perfect complement to play-action passing. Figure 8-2 illustrates a "Pro 8/Power right/Flood right pass." The wingback's pass route is almost identical to his blocking responsibility on the power right. In effect, he moves aggressively toward the safety, stalks him, and, when the safety reacts to him, he breaks into his pass route. If the pattern is executed well, the safety should be left behind wondering what happened.

Obviously, good play-action technique requires that all the receivers become "*deceivers.*" They must make the secondary believe that the play is a run; they must lure the safeties toward the backfield action and then embarrass them by breaking into their pass routes, often to find themselves *wide open*. The technique, when combined with the wingback's and the end's blocking responsibilities on running action, serves to weaken the safety's effectiveness on pass *and* run. His keys are never *really* reliable predictors of what the offense intends to do.

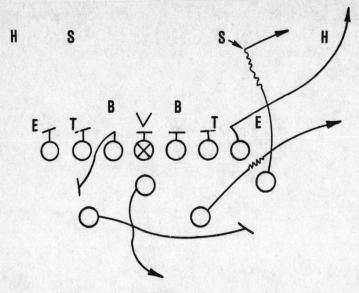

Figure 8-2

This is the primary reason why *play-action* passing is so important for most high school football teams. Most high school quarterbacks and, for that matter, most receivers have not developed the skills needed to sustain a strong passing offense, certainly not a strong *dropback* passing offense. The quarterback's abilities to read a defense, to know where his receivers are in relation to well-defended areas, and to pass the ball *to* the receiver as well as *away* from the defender just start to mature when he completes his final year of high school competition. Similarly, a receiver's abilities to get a defender off balance, to run a controlled pattern, and to establish a level of unspoken communication with the quarterback are difficult to teach young players because the coach probably is too preoccupied with the teaching of simple fundamentals.

The defensive secondary, on the other hand, must learn a few basic keys and two or three different coverages and must use their God-given talents to stay in position to prevent the pass reception. Usually, they have a clear advantage over the offense. This is not to say that coaching the defensive secondary is easy. But in relation to the many skills and techniques that quarterbacks and receivers must learn, the defensive secondary has the clear advantage in fundamentals and technique.

This is a big reason why most high school coaches spend much more of their time on the running game and less of it on passing. The important point to be made in this chapter, however, is that *play-action* passing eliminates the defense's edge; at times, it may even give the edge to the offense. The "why" is simple. The natural talents of the pass defenders are of little value to them if their keys are unreliable. If they are unable to read run or pass immediately, their reaction time will be slowed down. Play-action passing, therefore, not only establishes a team's passing game but complements its running game as well. In other words, if you burn the safety just once on the "Power right/Flood right pass," he will be less anxious to fill the next time the offense runs the "Power right."

The Pass Plays

We use set pass plays for two reasons. One, we believe in keeping it simple. Improvising patterns and combinations of patterns, sand lot style, leaves too much room for confusion in the huddle and, generally, for poor communication. Two, because the quarterback will be executing backfield fakes, he will be unable to watch his receivers as they move to the seams or to the open areas in the defense. The use of set plays lets him know where they will be or where they are likely to be when he completes his fakes and prepares to pass the ball. These two reasons, although important to *us,* are not unique to *our* offense. What *is* unique to our offense is our method of calling the pass plays, particularly the way we communicate assignments to each player on the field.

The assignments are communicated to each player through both the play call *and* the formation call. Each play assigns a particular pass route to each receiver, starting from the widest man on the side of the play call and ending with the widest man on the opposite side of the play call. *Where each player is located in the formation, therefore, will determine what pass route he is to run.* We have seven basic pass plays but can vary the receivers' responsibilities by changing the formation. We also can run each play to both the weak side and the strong side of the formation. So we get a lot of mileage from seven plays.

The Alabama

But let's eliminate the confusion. And rather than look at all seven pass plays, we will diagram and discuss four, the four that have been most successful for us. The first of these is the Alabama, which is illustrated in Figure 8-3. Notice that the formation is a "T 8." The Alabama assigns a "banana in" to the widest man to the side of the play call. It assigns a "slant out" to the second man in to the side of the play call. And it assigns a "hook in and slide" to the widest man on the opposite side of the play call. The "T 8," therefore, assigns the "banana in" to the wingback, the "slant out" to the right end, and the "hook in and slide" to the left end. So much for the basic play.

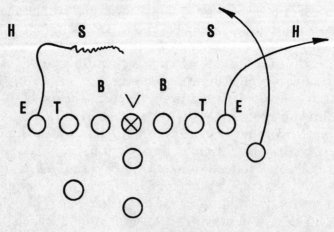

Figure 8-3

Next, as illustrated in Figure 8-4, look at the "T 8/*left* Alabama." Remember that the widest man *to the side of the play call* is assigned the "banana in," the second man in the "slant out," and so forth. The "T 8" is a "strong side right" formation, but the play call is to the left. This play call, then, will assign the "banana in" to the *left* end, the "slant out" to the left halfback (the second man in to the side of the play call), and the "hook in and slide" to the wingback (the widest man to the side of the line which is *opposite* the play call). This kind of variation gives us the chance to counteract pre-rotation or a similar defensive adjustment to the strong side of our formation. And remember, most of what we do is from play action, so we have the added advantage of confusing the daylights out of the secondary, especially if they pre-rotate to the strong side. Like a well-conceived complement of mis-direction plays, a complement of well-integrated play-action passes keeps the defense honest.

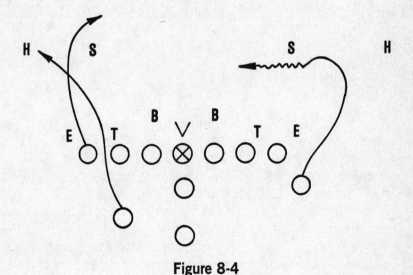

Figure 8-4

Finally, assume that you want to create a size mismatch between your tall right end and that short (but tough) onside safety. The play is still the right Alabama, but the formation call would be a "T 6-flex," as diagrammed in Figure 8-5. The right end is now the widest man to the side of the play call, and the wingback (now the slotback) is the second man in. Because of the formation call, therefore, their assignments have changed.

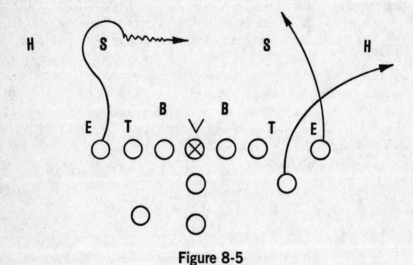

Figure 8-5

We have some other, equally simple, ways of exchanging assignments between receivers, but the purpose of this chapter is to introduce a few successful pass plays and then to explain their relationship to misdirection. It should be noted also that the play calls in combination with the formation call give us a lot of flexibility, and, although they may seem confusing at first, the system is really quite simple. Our kids learn it within the first week of practice. They may have questions regarding the particular pass routes within each play, but they learn the principles of the system very quickly.

The Others

The **Bradley** provides some of our long pass capability. Figure 8-6 illustrates the Bradley, the squiggly lines repre-

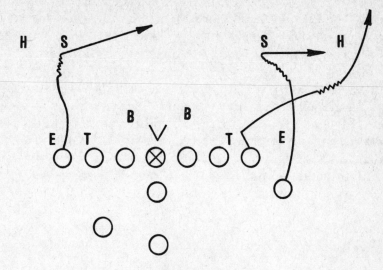

Figure 8-6

senting "stalking" techniques before breaking into pass routes. Obviously, each of the pass plays is successful to lesser or to greater degrees depending on its play-action complement. The Bradley is also dependent, perhaps more so than the other pass plays, on split-second timing between the passer and the deep receiver. For this reason, we conclude our passing drills with the Bradley. At this time, we instruct the deep receiver to start out slowly, in effect to simulate a stalking technique, then to run deep as fast as he can. At the same time, we instruct the quarterback to make his play-action fakes, to set his feet, and to "lay the ball out there" to let the receiver run under it. After two to three weeks of such timing, we find the combinations that work best, and we continue to work with them throughout the remainder of the year. These combinations prove to be real "game breakers," and they more than compensate for the small amount of time we invest in them.

The **Florida,** as illustrated in Figure 8-7, is a consistent ground gainer for us, our most reliable pass play. We use it exclusively with play action, unlike some of the other pass plays, which can be effective from drop back or sprint out action. The Florida from play action puts the onside safety in a real bind. The safety's primary key is likely to be the offensive left end, but he will have to pay at least *some* attention to the wingback, who will be stalking him. Once he realizes that the play is a pass, he probably will end up chasing the wingback to the outside. The other safety will be immobilized temporarily by the backfield action and then is likely to sprint to the deep middle of the field once he realizes PASS. His usual responsibility is to prevent any deep completions in the middle of the field and, like any good free safety, to help out once the ball is in the air.

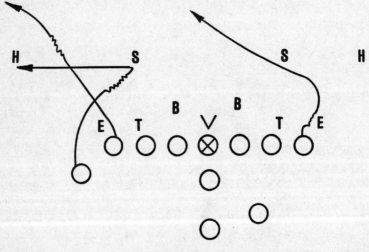

Figure 8-7

The right end is usually wide open. He normally finds himself several yards behind the onside safety and several yards underneath the offside safety. For that reason, we tell our quarterbacks to consider the right end to be the primary receiver. At times, when we are playing a team with aggressive and well-reacting linebackers, the quarterback may have to wait for the end to clear the linebackers, who will be dropping to the hook zones. Usually, however, the play action holds the linebackers so that they are no problem to us. But the quarterback should always be conscious of them, because they are the players in the best, maybe the only, position to stop the play. In a later section of this chapter, we will discuss the most effective play action to use with each pass play.

The final pass play to be discussed will be the **Georgia.** It is illustrated in Figure 8-8 and is used exclusively with counter action. Again, we find ourselves picking on a safety, and not without good reason. Safeties generally have the most difficult responsibilities of anyone in the secondary. They have important pass responsibilities but, more so than the defensive halfbacks, are also responsible for the run. They also are the players on the defense most likely to be embarrassed by the counter play, primarily because their key is drawing them away from the point of attack.

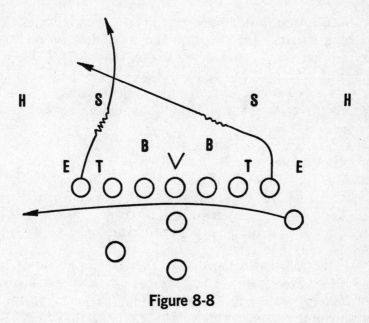

Figure 8-8

So the safeties tend to be very conscious of the counter play. To help them (we're nothing if not helpful!), we instruct our linemen on counter action/right or left Georgia to shout "Counter!" Once the onside safety sees the wingback moving down the line of scrimmage and hears someone shout

"Counter," he is likely to freeze, if only for a split second. And that's all we want him to do.

We beat one of our most talented and well-coached opponents one year with just this play. After having run several moderately successful counter plays late in the game, we called a "Power counter at 5 action/left Georgia" on a second and four situation and watched the left end catch the ball for the winning touchdown with *no one* within twenty yards of him. As with misdirection running plays, the more aggressive the defensive personnel and the more well-coached they are, the more success a team will have with play-action passing, especially if used with misdirection.

Play Action with Misdirection

Play-action passing and misdirection make for a nasty combination. The misdirection keeps the defense confused; the play-action passing keeps them scared. The offensive potential to throw deep on any given play keeps the secondary honest, even a little hesitant. Such potential does wonders for the ground game. Even the short passes can be big gainers.

We won a state championship with the Alabama. We had been playing a well-coached, hard-nosed football team that was doing a lot of slanting and looping with the defensive line, so we decided to go right at them with a succession of quick openers, in our terminology, quicks at three and four. On occasion we would vary the attack with an option or a quick slant trap, but the quick opener seemed to be getting us consistently good yardage, three and four yeards at a crack.

The safeties, even the defensive halfbacks, were coming up harder and harder, tackling the ball and doing whatever they could to stop our progress. On a second and three situation, somewhere near our opponent's thirty yard line, we called a "Pro 8/Quick slant trap at 1 action/Right Alabama." As illustrated in Figure 8-9, the play call is a natural if the secondary is conscious of the run. The wingback and the right end run pass routes which are identical to their downfield blocking responsibilities. The quick slant trap action, because the ball is concealed by the quarterback's body during the fake, does not show PASS too soon. In this situation it did just what we wanted it to do. The right end was wide open for the reception, which resulted in the winning touchdown.

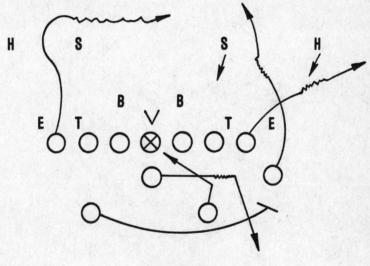

Figure 8-9

A Day Late and a Dollar Short

We went thirteen and zero that year and owed much of it to the Bradley pattern and to a passing combination that learned how to click on the deep one. Our offensive right end, as a matter of fact, scored or set up so many key touchdowns with his receptions that the Chicago sports writers began to refer to him as "Deep 6." The play which was so successful for him, as illustrated in Figure 8-10, was the "Crossfire at 8 action/Right Bradley." Much of the play's success resulted from our extensive use of crossfire action and the excellent faking ability of our backfield. In addition, the line had

mastered the "fire out" block, so well that the secondary had
very few keys to rely on, especially early in the play. Obviously, as the play progressed, the secondary recognized
what was happening, but they always seemed a day late and
a dollar short.

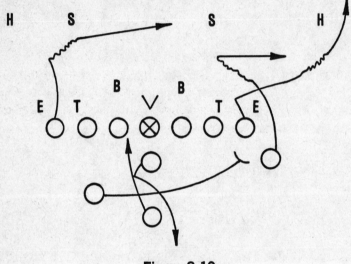

Figure 8-10

The initial confusion of the secondary is one reason why
the pass is never really a deep one. We call it a "bomb"
sometimes and generally tend to think of it as such, but it
really isn't. It usually ends up being a thirty to thirty-five
yard pass. An advantage most of the time, such a short
"bomb" can be a disadvantage at others. Obviously, the ball
has to be passed when the receiver is open, and he is likely to
be *most* open two to three steps after he makes his move into
his pass route. Play-action passing, because of stalking technique and backfield faking, takes a little longer to set up
than conventional passing attacks. Long passes, therefore,
tend to be shorter than from drop back or sprint out action,

even though the quarterback is prepared to release the ball sooner when he simply drops back.

In high school, this fact is a clear advantage because most high school quarterbacks do not have the strength required to complete fifty or sixty yard passes, even occasionally. Play-action, therefore, provides yet another dimension for the high school passing attack. At the same time, the relative shortness of the pass, especially early in the game, can cause stronger quarterbacks to overthrow their receivers. This is just one of the reasons why we time this pattern so often and why we encourage our quarterbacks to "lay the ball out there" in order to let the receivers run under it. Such a technique provides for better timing and makes the ball easier to catch.

The Florida with More Crossfire Action

The Bradley and the Florida are diagrammed with crossfire action because it is an excellent series for us, probably because of its simple misdirection. Certainly, other series are possible. The success of the series from which play action is run, however, in large part will determine the success of the pass attempt. "Complement" is still the key word.

The **Florida** is a more precise pass than the Bradley. The ball must be delivered quickly and accurately to the receiver. The play-action fakes, always important, are especially important with the Florida as well as with the other short pass plays. The defenders who are most likely to cause problems for the short passes are the linebackers. That is one reason we like to run crossfire action. Our fullback tends to be focal within our offense, so he has good "holding power." He attracts a lot of attention from the linebackers.

Already indicated in this chapter, the right end, as illustrated in Figure 8-11, is the primary receiver. The play action should hold the linebackers; the patterns in the right half of the secondary should clear the area for the right end;

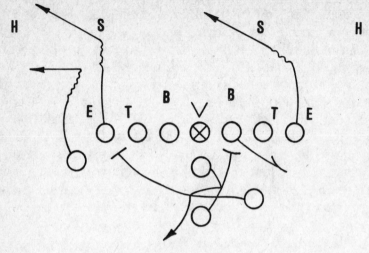

Figure 8-11

and the offside safety probably will be dropping to the deep middle zone. If he does not, the play is still a completion if the ball is thrown with moderate accuracy.

The pass play which is probably most effective against the safeties is the **Georgia**, as illustrated in Figure 8-12, because we run it only with counter action. And the counter action we use most often is the crossfire counter at five or six. Of the several counter plays we run, the crossfire counter seems to be the most immobilizing for the defense, probably because of its organized confusion. The fullback starts in one direction, then veers to another to fill for the tackle. The home halfback is faking into an off-tackle hole. And the wingback is racing down the line of scrimmage to take a fake from the quarterback. In addition, this is the only counter play that provides three "tight" fakes behind the offensive center. When combined with our lineman shouting "Counter," the result is a thoroughly confusing experience for the secondary, especially for the safeties, who already may have been embarrassed by the counter play.

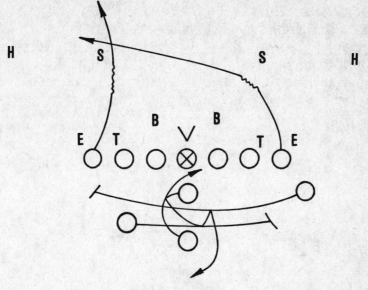

Figure 8-12

Play-Action Screens

Because much of our offense is run between the offensive tackles, we run into a lot of defenses that crash the defensive ends. By so doing, they believe that they can shut down the counter plays and stack up the power play. Sometimes they do. Usually, however, we just run inside the crashing end on the counter plays and cut them down and run to the outside on the power plays. But our play-action passes are additional incentive for the ends to close down hard. After the safeties have been burned once or twice, opposing coaches are likely to emphasize a strong pass rush, especially from the ends, where slashing techniques complement the running defense anyway.

Once we see the ends closing down hard, especially if we want to get them to back off on our running plays, we can

call a "Crossfire at 8 action/Screen right." Figure 8-13 diagrams the left halfback's path against a hard-charging defensive end. It also re-illustrates the complementary relationships among our basic series, misdirection, and play-action
passing. Everything looks like everything else. That's the
beauty of play-action passing.

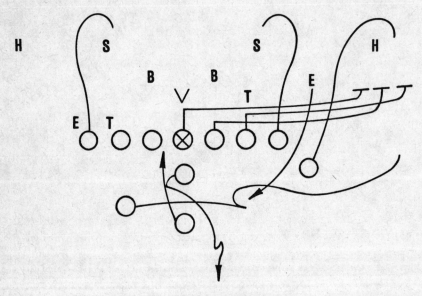

Figure 8-13

To illustrate this point further, Figure 8-14 emphasizes
the same formation and the same backfield action, but with
a screen left. The play is a little sneakier than the screen
right from the crossfire at eight action because the fullback
can lose himself in the middle of the line before releasing to
the flat to catch the pass. It can be a *very* sneaky play if the
quarterback drops and fakes a screen pass first to the
halfback, then turns and throws a left screen pass to the
fullback. A creative coach can even use misdirection *screens.*
    Finally, if the offense has a talented quarterback with
the poise to find any one of the three potential receivers, the

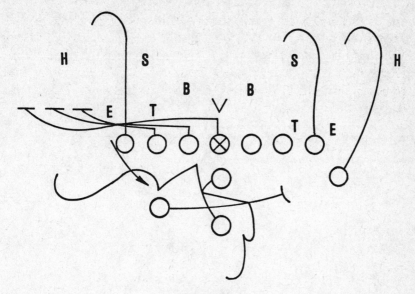

Figure 8-14

crossfire counter enables the offense to run a triple screen. Figure 8-15 illustrates the "T 8/Crossfire counter at 5 action/ Screen left." As diagrammed, it could be called "T 8/Crossfire counter at 5 action/Triple screen," and the team simply would rely on the quarterback to pick out the open man. This, however, is a very difficult task for *any* quarterback, so when we use counter action we normally throw the screen pass to the counter back. He is the most likely of the three to be open because the defense quickly avoids our counter back once they see that he does not have the ball. In addition, the threat of a middle screen tends to hold the middle linebacker, thereby opening up the screen to the counter back, especially if the line is hard-charging.

All these screen passes serve to highlight the complementary nature and the internal consistency of the offense. We can call the screen pass to compensate for a hard-charging defensive line. But while we are doing this, we are conditioning the safeties to remember the screen pass the next time we want to run the Georgia pattern. If all goes well

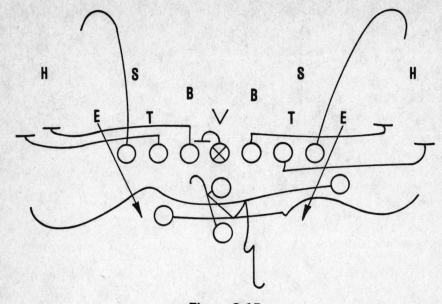

Figure 8-15

and we watch the defense's reactions carefully, we can keep them off balance throughout most of the game.

A Couple of Quick Hints

Before we summarize this chapter, we should mention three techniques that are fundamental to a successful screen pass. They may be obvious to the veteran coach, but, because of their importance, we will risk insulting your intelligence.

1. The quarterback should be instructed to look at his deep receivers first. They are all instructed to run 17 to 18 yard hook patterns. The hook patterns clear the zones for the screen and still enable the potential receivers to come back to block for the ball carrier. If any of the onside receivers is *wide open*, the quarterback is instructed to forget the screen and to throw it to the open receiver downfield. This has happened only once in the past ten years, but the technique

keeps the quarterback looking downfield, in essence to "sell" the screen.

2. The quarterback must never try to lead the receiver. The ball must be thrown at the receiver's numbers. Few backs can set up to block a hard-charging end, sneak past him, get some depth behind the screen, and still muster up enough steam to catch a ball which is thrown a couple of yards ahead of them. Besides, the receiver should be somewhat flat-footed when he catches the ball. If he were to catch the ball on the run, he might run past his screen. We have seen this happen several times. But worse, we have seen an unthinking quarterback try to lead the receiver only to throw the ball on the ground in front of him—with nothing but open prairie between the screen and the end zone.

3. The back receiving the screen should always release an onrushing lineman to his outside and sneak out to the flat *behind* him. If he releases the lineman to his inside, the route to the quarterback is shorter. Of equal importance, the receiver will be releasing in front of the lineman, who is likely to see him and to follow him to the flat and break up the play. Any receiver, even the backs on screen passes, have to be pass "deceivers," always suggesting the possibility of something other than what they are doing at the moment.

Let's Wrap It Up

No chapter on play-action passing is complete without a brief discussion of the bootleg. Because it will be mentioned again in the next chapter, the specifics of its execution need not be mentioned here. For now, it is sufficient to emphasize the fake between the quarterback and the running back, as illustrated in Figure 8-16. Because the onside safety probably will be keying the home halfback, the fake will have to hold him in order to open the zone to the deep outside. It is also important if the quarterback is to get outside the defensive right end, either to run (if he has daylight) or to pass the ball. The play call is a "Pro 8/Power bootleg pass at 7" and surprises even us at times when we see

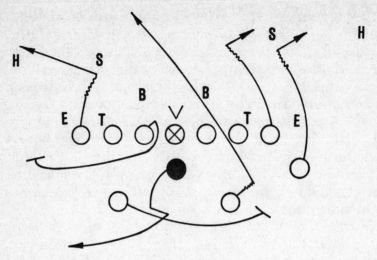

Figure 8-16

the fullback wide open in the middle of the field. The one or two steps he takes to his right simulates his blocking path on the power right. His next few steps are shielded by the activity in the middle of the line. By the time he breaks into his pass route, the secondary has started much of its rotation and often will simply disregard the fullback. More of the bootleg will be mentioned in the next chapter.

The bootleg, especially within our offense, suggests a very important point about beating a zone defense. Any variation of speed or of depth of penetration into the secondary will make the defensive zones larger than they are normally. As long as the potential receivers remain relatively close to one another, the pass defenders have an easier time covering them. Once the receivers vary their speed and/or penetrate the secondary at different depths, the zones become larger, and the secondary has to cover more ground, unless they are covering man-to-man, which is unlikely in high school. This is the primary reason why the fullback is sometimes so wide open on the bootleg. He enters the secondary more slowly and at a different time, a time when the safeties already have started to cover someone else. Even if they see the fullback emerge from the middle of the line, they are likely to think that someone else will pick him up.

Other characteristics of play-action passing warrant some additional mention. This chapter has emphasized the need for play-action passing in high school and has discussed some important characteristics of such a passing attack. The most obvious characteristic is the complementary relationship that exists between the running and the passing attacks. Each resembles the other, a fact which causes the defensive secondary, particularly the safeties, a lot of trouble. If the offense executes well, the defense can never be certain what the play will be. It may be the basic play; it may be misdirection; or it may be a pass. When the defense finally does determine what the play is, it is often too late for them to do anything about it. They may be as fundamentally sound as any team in the area, perhaps even better than you, but if you can keep 'em guessing, their fundamental superiority will not do them any good.

Play-action passing also holds the linebackers. Because they are unable to get into their zones quickly enough to help the secondary, the zones for the safeties and halfbacks are larger still. When combined with the receivers entering the zones at different depths and at variable speeds, the whole picture gets tougher and tougher for the secondary. Now add their uncertainty regarding pass or run. The end result is not only a much improved passing attack but one that will do much to improve the effectiveness of your running attack as well.

9

Motion and the
Misdirection Offense

So Who Needs Motion?

A good offensive football team, well-groomed in fundamentals and operating with a well-conceived offense, may
never need to use motion. Some football teams are so well
organized and so disciplined and draw from such large pools
of talented athletes that winning records each year become
routine. They may not win conference or state champion-
ships every year, but the *habit* of winning, especially when
combined with the needed tools to do it, helps to sustain a
successful program, one which they may be disinclined to
change. Such programs really do exist, as dreamlike as they
may sound!

For the rest of us, however, even those of us with well-
conceived offenses and fundamentally sound players, the
sustained challenge of equally well-prepared opposition
forces us to use *all* the tools of the trade. And motion, when
used in the right circumstances, can be an exceptionally

effective tool. Being a tool, its effectiveness is dependent upon how and why it is used. Following are the primary reasons that *we* use motion.

We use motion so infrequently that most of our opponents are never prepared for it when we use it. Normally, we wait for a big game to spring it on someone, but occasionally we'll use it early in the season on a relatively easy opponent in order to practice it "under fire." So when we use it, we plan, initially at least, to gang up on one segment of an unprepared defense, usually the outside on running action and occasionally the defensive halfback on passing action.

Most defenses position players and plan adjustments and stunts based upon the alignment of offensive personnel. The easiest way to determine defensive "balance" is to count the number of players on either side of the offensive center and then be sure to determine that the defense has a similar number. Figure 9-1 illustrates the Fullhouse formation; the line divides the team in half. A quick count reveals five and a half players on each side of the formation, the center, quarterback, and fullback counted as half positions for each side. The formation is balanced.

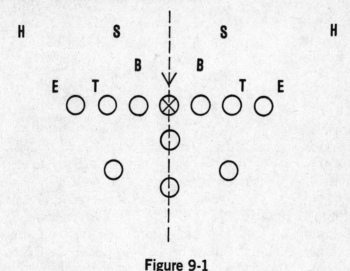

Figure 9-1

So is the defense. Considering the noseman as a half position on each side, another quick count reveals five and a half defensive men on each side of the offensive center. All else being equal, both teams are at even strength. Figure 9-2 reveals an obvious *im*balance between offensive and defensive alignments. The side to the right of the offensive center contains the equivalent of six and a half players, the side to the left, four and a half. Obviously, the defensive team will have to adjust in order to compensate for the offense's numerical superiority on the right side of the line of scrimmage.

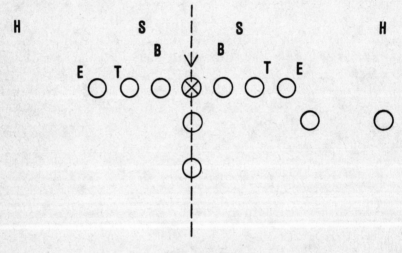

Figure 9-2

If *motion* creates the numerical imbalance, the defensive team may be unable to adjust quickly enough to equalize an obvious offensive strength. When finally they *do* adjust, the offense probably will have achieved four things. One, they will have caused the opposing team's secondary to doubt their *planned* defense for the game. Two, the adjustments they make may eliminate their stunts or their use of a monster, or at least, force them into alignments that they haven't practiced. Three, the adjustments made by the secondary will provide immediately obvious clues regarding probable pass coverage. And, four, the offense will have set up misdirection plays to be used *against* the motion. Some of these advantages will be considered in a later section of this chapter.

For now, however, look at figure 9-3. The formation is a "T 7." The jagged line represents the wingback's flat motion before the snap of the ball. By the time the ball is snapped, motion has transformed the formation from a T 7 to a Wing 8 and has created an imbalance between offensive and defensive alignments, the offense having a one-man advantage to their right. The fullback power right, then becomes an effective play. So also might the quarterback sprint-out run at 8.

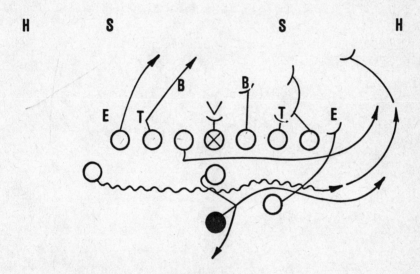

Figure 9-3

Certainly this strategy presents nothing new to the veteran coach. Such a tactic is relatively commonplace in high school football and, as any defensive coordinator knows, requires a few simple adjustments in the secondary to counteract the offense's attempt at imbalance. The strategy can be very effective, however, if the defense employs a 5-2 monster to the side of the wingback. The flat motion and a running play away from the monster can be a good

strategy, but the flat motion and the time it requires allow
the defense to adjust. So a better play, versus a 5-2 monster
as diagrammed in Figure 9-4, might be the "T 7/motion
right/crossfire trap at 4." The play hits quickly and provides
simple misdirection. It not only runs away from the monster
but momentarily confuses the linebackers, who probably
will be cross keying the home backs. In addition, if the
defensive line is slanting away from the wingback in order to
shut down inside crossfire action and if the linebackers are
scraping against the slanting line, the "motion/crossfire trap
at 4" is particularly effective.

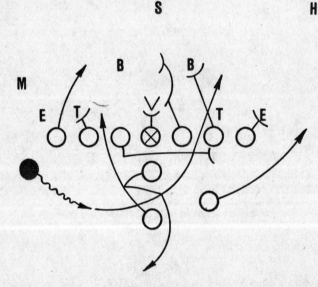

Figure 9-4

Most effective, however, is a double wing versus the
team that develops its stunts or positions its monster in
relationship to the strength of your offensive formation. The
double wing (or the double slot) with motion reveals no
strong side or weak side in the formation and allows the
team to run its entire offense. It heightens the guessing game
between teams but allows the offense to continue running its
favorite plays without giving away obvious tendencies. The

"Double wing/Motion right/Inside belly option at 8," as illustrated in Figure 9-5, can run away from the monster or, as with the previous example, can confuse the keys of the linebackers and secondary and shake the confidence of a slanting defensive line. Once their confidence is shaken, they are likely to play us "straight up" and to become more susceptible to misdirection.

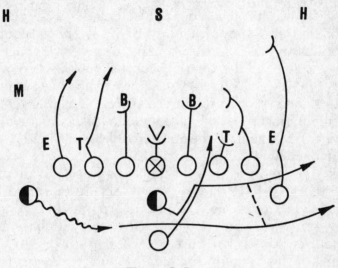

Figure 9-5

Timing Is Important

Our execution of motion is quite simple. Its simplicity is based primarily on our cadence: "Down/Green ... Go." We simplified the cadence for three reasons. One, we wanted our players on each play to concentrate only on the execution of their assignments, not on *when* to fire out of their stances. Two, we wanted to eliminate off-side penalties. Three, we needed an efficient format when we wanted to use motion.

The simplified cadence has been very successful for us. It has helped in all three areas. One disadvantage has been the defense's ability to use the same snap signal, but it has been only a minor disadvantage because we also have

incorporated a "dead call" into our bag of tricks. Periodically
throughout the game, but especially when we need five easy
yards, we'll tell the quarterback to call a "dead call" in the
huddle. This instructs the team *not to move* after "Down/
Green ... Go." It usually results in a five yard gain for us. If
the defense does not go offside, the quarterback simply
repeats the cadence and we run the play as previously
determined in the huddle.

This simplified cadence also enables us to run motion
with a minimum of confusion. If the play requires flat
motion (review Figure 9-3), we instruct the wingback to start
his motion on the quarterback's signal, usually a simple
movement of the foot. Our quarterback then pauses one
count and starts his regular cadence. On regular motion, the
wingback is instructed to be set for a full count, then to go on
"Down." By the time the quarterback says "Green ... Go," the
wingback will have been in the approximate area of his
regular home position, so the timing is quite simple. Over
the years we have had to devote very little practice time to
our use of motion, so it can be incorporated into our offense
any time we want it. Obviously, you will have to make
whatever adjustments are necessary to fit it into your system. The key principle on regular motion, however, is that it
seems *most* effective when clued in to the cadence. *Visual*
signals just seem to get in the way.

Misdirect the Motion

Next, let's assume that, like most good defenses, the
opposing team adjusts to the motion. They probably will
make the primary adjustments somewhere in the secondary,
but they may also have to eliminate some of their line stunts,
especially if the offense has gone to a double wing. Regardless of what they do with their defensive stunts, the opposing
team will be highly susceptible to misdirection after the
offense has hit them with several motion plays.

The primary reasons for their susceptibility involve the
adjustments they might make in the secondary and their

tendency to react in the general direction of the motion, especially if the offense has used motion successfully to overload a defensive zone. Look once more at Figure 9-3. The wingback's flat motion right establishes an imbalance to the offense's right side and, especially after a few successful running or passing plays in that direction, will force the defense to adjust. A standard adjustment involves the secondary's "sliding up to, but no more than a man over" in the direction of the motion. Most defenders won't even move that much because of their reluctance to move before the ball is snapped, but *most* will move at least half a man over and, when they see the backfield action, will tend to continue their movement in the same direction.

Misdirection against motion, especially from a double wing, puts the defense in a real bind. One, they have a built-in tendency to concentrate on the area to the side of the motion. Two, the linebackers and at least one of the safeties have only one home back to key, and he's moving in the general direction of the motion man. This latter part is

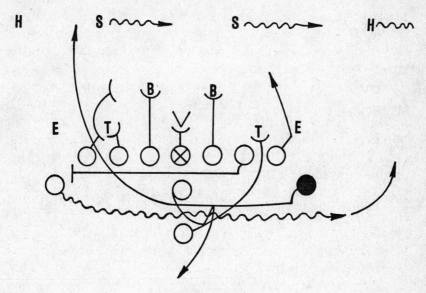

Figure 9-6

especially effective against well-coached defenses who rely heavily on keys. Defensive players on such teams will watch the fullback, primarily because he's the only player "at home" but also because he usually brings the defense to the point of attack.

Figure 9-6, a complement to the fullback power illustrated in Figure 9-3, provides an excellent example of misdirecting against motion. The wavy lines in the secondary illustrate the defender's *probable* adjustment to flat motion. The right defensive halfback will remain stationary because he is likely to be assigned man-to-man coverage of the offensive left end. The "Double Wing/Flat motion right/ Fullback power counter at 5" is a natural, almost frustrating enough to cause the opposing coach to spike his Gatorade. His adjustment to prevent an imbalance on one side of the line of scrimmage has resulted in a positional weakness on the other.

Sometimes You Just Can't Win

Defenses may be tempted to make similar adjustments once either of the wingbacks moves into regular motion. Figure 9-7 illustrates a "Double Wing/Motion Right/Inside belly counter at 5." If the "Motion right/Inside belly option right" has been successful, even moderately successful, the defense is likely to get into their pursuit paths early, too early to adjust to the counter play. The play is easy to execute, little different from the same play when the left halfback is in his home position.

Even if unsuccessful, a well-executed counter play against the motion prevents the defense from adjusting too quickly to what will be an offensive advantage. Their hesitation is just what the offense wants.

Turn the Monster Every Which Way but Loose

Figure 9-4 illustrated one example (there are many others) of how to use motion to run away from a monster.

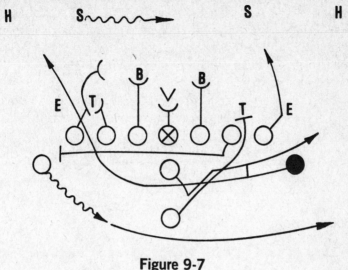

Figure 9-7

Football coaches have devised a number of excellent ways to counteract the defensive strategy of anticipating the direction of the play. Running away from the monster is not particularly new. But motion away from the monster in order to run the ball back to where he was originally provides another dimension to unpredictability.

The double wing with motion takes away much of the defense's planning because it does not present a strong or a weak side. So defensive alignments based on tendencies by formation are generally useless. *Misdirection* further confuses the defense by throwing another monkey wrench into their planning once they make their adjustments to the motion. The play illustrated in Figure 9-8 represents an excellent complement to the defensive adjustment of having the monster follow the motion man, a fairly common adjustment. The play is a "Double Wing/Motion Right/Crossfire Counter at 5." The monster may be anticipating a "Crossfire trap at 4," as in Figure 9-4, or he may be chasing any one of several plays which capitalized on the imbalance formerly created by the motion away.

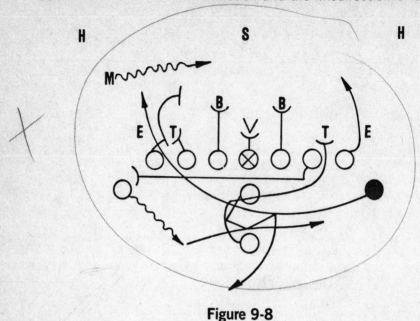

Figure 9-8

Whatever his reasons, the monster, at least on this particular play, is running *away* from the point of attack. Doing this two or three times is all that is normally required to create a "flat-footed monster." We're not altogether sure what a "flat-footed monster" looks like, but we're pretty sure that it mutters only four-letter words and has a red face.

Speaking of Red Faces ...

Red faces reflect both embarrassment and anger. A monster running away from the point of attack is an embarrassed football player, and a safety who is unable to get in on the action is an angry one. The opportunity to flood a zone is one of the main advantages of motion, and it does much to keep the offside safety out of the action. Again looking at flat motion, Figure 9-9 illustrates a "T 7/Flat motion right/FB power flood right pass." The play action complements the fullback power, which previously was diagrammed in Figure 9-3. Although the flat motion will provoke an adjustment in the secondary which probably will put the offside safety in a

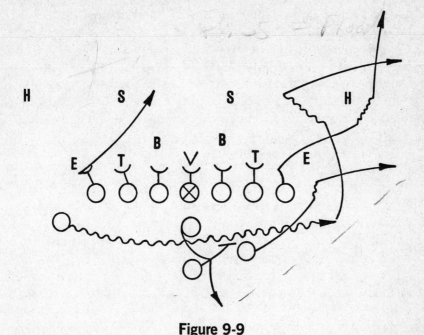

Figure 9-9

position to help out near the "flooded zone," the play action should immobilize the safeties long enough to free both deep receivers to the outside.

An obvious key to the success of the play, the motion man's "stalk" on the onside safety helps to immobilize *both* safeties. The right halfback can't be in a hurry to break into his pass route, nor can the quarterback or the fullback rush the play. If just one player gets too anxious and shows "pass" too soon, the play is likely to be just another pass attempt. With everyone doing his job, however, it becomes a complement to the running game and an important part of the team's unpredictability.

Hit 'Em Where They Ain't

Once the safety starts moving with the motion man, especially if we've been able to flood a zone or to run with success to his offside, he can leave a fairly sizable gap in the secondary. Flat motion generally is the best way to get him to move, but once he's been conditioned to slide with motion, he's likely to react to any kind of motion in the backfield. So the "Double wing/Motion right/Crossfire bootleg pass at 7," which is illustrated in Figure 9-10, provides the misdirection needed to transform a normally effective defensive adjustment into a positional weakness.

A few points are important if the play is to pick up yardage. We like to reverse pull the center versus the even front and the onside guard versus the odd. The reverse pull has the lineman take his first step in the direction of the backfield action, then pivot to become the quarterback's personal protector. Because the guard will be vacating a particularly vulnerable area in the offensive line, the fullback, if the linebacker is coming, will have to make contact with the linebacker with his *inside shoulder* before releasing into his pass route. He can't take the easy way out and simply release a blitzing linebacker to his inside. If he does, the linebacker will be on top of the quarterback before he

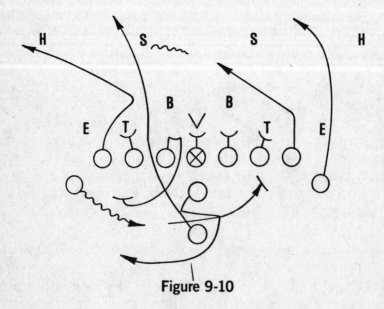

Figure 9-10

can take four steps. So we tell the fullback to keep any penetration to his inside before he releases into the secondary. The play action, if executed well, will make it easier for him to do so.

From that point, all he does is "sneak out." While he's executing his crossfire fake, he's been instructed to look for any penetration and to watch the movement of the secondary. He may delay in the hole after his fake for a half count while he's watching the secondary. After he does so, he "eases into the secondary," then breaks hard to the deep outside. At that point, the defensive halfback is in a lot of trouble, especially if the onside safety is sliding over with the motioned wingback.

Let's Wrap It Up

Motion accomplishes many things. It provides a predictable way to get the secondary out of position in order to hit them with misdirection. But we certainly don't want a steady diet of misdirection, or it isn't misdirection, so we use motion to create a numerical advantage on either side of the center. Then, when the defense adjusts, we throw their adjustments into the computer and determine the best misdirection play to use against them. Knowing how and when to use misdirection can make you a real pain in the neck.

Defenses enjoy playing against a predictable offense. They can look at certain formations and have a good idea of where the ball is likely to go. When they have that kind of confidence about an opposing team, they can organize their defensive stunts according to the offense's alignment. And if the offensive alignment remains a reliable indication of where the ball is to be run, the offense is in real trouble, and they will remain in real trouble until they eliminate those clues.

One good way to eliminate them is to run from the double wing. One of the major advantages of motion as described in this chapter, when run from the double wing, is that it lets you run your entire offense without giving any tendencies by formation. The defense that is prepared to slant into the wing or to "scrape off" away from the tight end is stymied by the balance of the double wing. The use of motion further confuses the secondary, each of whom have to be prepared to make some kind of an adjustment. Finally, the use of misdirection *againt the motion* caps off a thoroughly frustrating day for the defense.

Motion provides other advantages, clues regarding the kind of coverage the secondary may be using, for example. To high school offenses and to high school quarterbacks, however, such clues, although potentially valuable, are not as useful as they might be to pro teams. Pro teams will use a variety of pass defenses, and any insight to be gained by the offense is helpful, during or after the play. But in high school, because of the limited number of pass defenses used, the same insight is generally reliable for the entire game.

So motion can be helpful in learning about pass defenses, in flooding a zone, or in creating numerical superiority to one side of the center. But its primary strength in high school, at least to us, is that it enables us to run from an offensive set that allows us to run our entire offense, the way we like to—without giving away vital clues to a well-prepared defense.

All this means that the smart football team is going to know its tendencies and to do whatever needs to be done to counteract the planning of the defense. That is the subject of the next chapter.

10

Scout Yourself:
Never Give a Defense
an Even Break

Know Your Tendencies

A key principle governing the use of misdirection is to call it when the defense gangs up on the offense's basic plays. And defenses are more likely to try to gang up when they feel that they can predict reliably what the offense is going to do. Once they have made their predictions, they can adjust the positions of linemen and linebackers from standard alignments to flexed alignments, stacks, gap stacks, offset nosemen, and the like. Or they can maintain standard alignments but inside scrape the 5-2 backers with the noseman or outside scrape them with the tackles. Or they can slant the line in a particular direction or "deal" with individual linemen. Books have been written about the dizzying array of stunts available to a good defensive coach, so a great many variations are possible. And most good defensive coaches will employ their stunts strategically; only occasionally will they be used randomly.

The greater the predictability of the offensive team, the more enthusiastically the opponent enters into the prepara-

171

tion of his defensive game plan and, as a result, the more confidently his players will execute their assignments. The wise offensive coach, therefore, wants little more than to stifle his opposing coach's enthusiasm and to rattle his players' confidence. Misdirection is the answer. Misdirection is going to help whenever it is used because it always provides the advantages already enumerated earlier. But it will be especially effective if the offensive coach does his homework—on himself.

Routinely scout yourself. Look at yourself as an opponent would look at you. Identify your tendencies by down and distance and even by field position. Most important, determine what you do from each of your favorite formations. This latter tendency is by far the most important, primarily because it will determine what your opponent will do to adjust his defenses to stop you. Once he makes his adjustments, your use of misdirection to counteract them will take all the fun out of his game plan. It also will force him to re-think the value of his alignments and stunts and, perhaps, to discard them in favor of his more standard defense, one with which he and *you* are more familiar—and more comfortable. Then continue to use misdirection to keep him honest.

But before any of this can happen (we'll discuss some specific examples later in this chapter), the offensive coach must be familiar with his tendencies. A key word in this book is unpredictability. Misdirection by itself will not guarantee unpredictability. Some coaches, based on the desire to sequence their plays, may use misdirection *predictably*. A coach, for example, may fall into the predictable pattern of calling two or three power plays to the outside, followed by a power slant trap at one or a power counter at five. Once the defense determines this tendency, especially if it corresponds to tendencies by down and distance, they will be able to anticipate the call by making any one of several defensive adjustments.

The key, then, is to avoid predictability. Our scouting format has become so streamlined within the past few years that it serves our purposes well. It has allowed us not only to gather important information about our opponents but also to look at ourselves routinely in order to find out what we're doing.

The Scouting Format

Our scouting format capitalizes on our formation-calling system. Its basic simplicity and the flexibility it affords us are advantages in the huddle as well as in the stands when we scout an opponent. To understand the format, a quick review of our formation-calling system is necessary. We run our offense from several basic formations, each of which is diagrammed in Figure 10-1. Each has been given an arbitrary name and is easily learned by our players. These formations are basic to our offense, although we can use others. Figure 10-2 illustrates a few more formations: the Wishbone, the Shotgun, the Double Wing, the Double Slot, and the "Trips Right" formations. They are illustrated because on occasion our opponents will use them against us. Other formations certainly are possible. The point is, however, that all the coach needs to do is to give each formation he sees or uses a name, and the rest of the format is easy. As with most of the formations in Figure 10-2, his job is already complete, because the Shotgun, the Double Wing, the Double Slot, and the Trips Right have no variations.

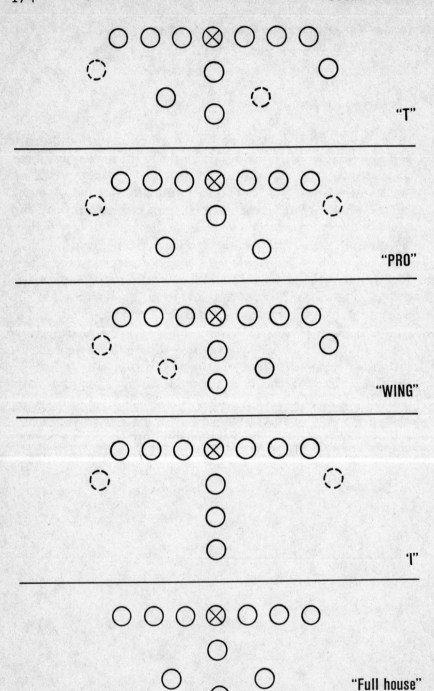

Figure 10-1

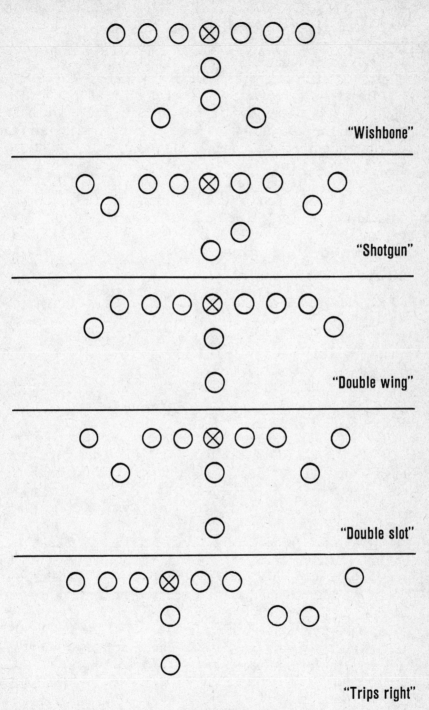

"Wishbone"

"Shotgun"

"Double wing"

"Double slot"

"Trips right"

Figure 10-2

Names and Numbers Are All It Takes

It is so easy that it is complete when the coach assigns a number to each lineman's normal position and to certain additional spots along the line of scrimmage. As indicated in Figure 10-3, the left end is designated a five, the left tackle a three, and the left guard a one, and the center a zero, and so on down the line of scrimmage, the right side receiving the even numbers. In addition, a spot approximately one yard to the outside of the offensive left end is designated the seven position; another spot anywhere from ten to fifteen yards outside the left end is designated the nine position. Conversely, the eight and the ten positions are located similarly to the outside of the right end.

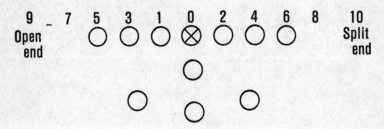

Figure 10-3

A final point involves the positioning of the ends. If we want the left end split, we initiate the formation call with the term "Open." If we want to split the right end, we *conclude* the formation call with the term "Split." If neither of these terms is called when we designate the formation, both ends are tight. If we want to "flex" either end, i.e., position him approximately three to five yards outside his tackle, we initiate the call with the term "Flex" for the left end or conclude it with "Flex" for the right end. We use the flex positions so infrequently that we see no reason to use distinct terms for each end. That's really all there is to it.

When combined with the names of the backfield sets, the numbers and the end designations enable us to identify quickly any formation we see while scouting, or for that matter, to call any of the over three hundred formations that we might use during a game. The players pick up the system with amazing ease. All they have to remember is what each backfield set looks like and that the odd numbers in the call instruct the left halfback where to position himself; the even numbers instruct the right halfback. Finally, if the call begins with either "Open" or "Flex," it refers to the left end; if it concludes with either "Split" or "Flex," it refers to the right end.

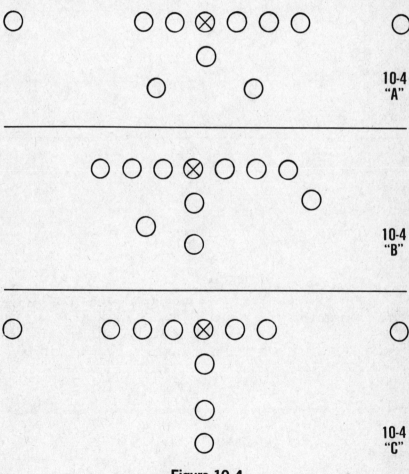

Figure 10-4

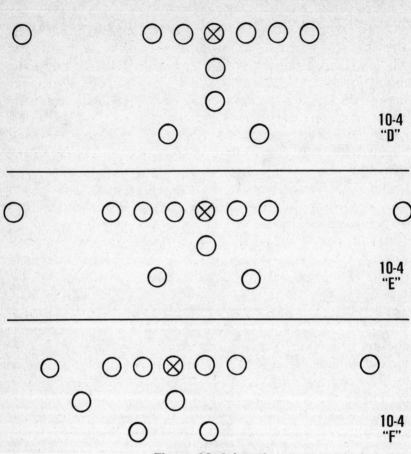

Figure 10-4 (cont)

Figure 10-4 illustrates six different formations, all of which currently are very popular, either in college or in the pros. Look at all six and try to name each before you read the answers which follow. You already are very familiar with one of them. We have used it throughout the book. The terms are, starting from the top left hand corner, the "Open-Pro 10," a very popular pro formation; the "T 8," a formation that we use very often: the "I 9-Split," a popular formation used by many colleges; the "Open-Wishbone," one of the basic alignments for the triple option; the "Pro 9-Split," another popular pro formation; and the "Flex-Pro 5-Split," an interesting concoction that no one seems wild about but that someday may be fun to throw at someone. The possible combinations, especially as more backfield sets are introduced, are endless.

We feel that our crossfire, belly, power, and quick series also describe most of what we might see other teams run while we scout them. Certainly, they use different designations, but the backfield action and the general play sequencing seem to be fundamentally the same. If they do run from series fundamentally different from our own, we'll give it a name on the spot, diagram one play to show the basic backfield action, and continue to simply write down the names of successive plays. Most of the plays that we see, however, are much like ours or are simple variations of our own, so we have never had much of a problem with this part of the scouting format.

As a matter of fact, we have never had much trouble with any part of the scouting format because it is so easy and quick. Our staff, while scouting a triple option team, for example, might observe a "Wishbone-Split/Inside Belly at 5." The scouting report would contain "W-S/IB5." Such a format certainly involves an economy of words and allows us enough time, even if only one or two coaches are scouting, to look for other things. While our colleagues from other schools are drawing X's and O's and are diagramming backfield action, we are writing down "W-S/IB5" and are watching for traps, cross blocks, finesse blocks, or any of several insights into what makes the team tick.

An added advantage of this format is that with a few simple modifications, the scouting reports for an upcoming opponent can be computerized, and his tendencies can be identified and systematized in a matter of seconds. We have saved much valuable time in preparation for an opponent by letting the computer do most of the work. By not having to break down the scouting reports, we can devote more time to the analysis of our offense, especially if we scout *ourselves* and also crank that information into the computer.

A Good Look at Yourself

Even without the use of a computer, our scouting format enables us, especially before big games, to take a good, hard look at what we have been doing. Because our lower-level coaches play their games before we do, most of them do the scouting on our game days, including the one who scouts our game. Aside from the benefit we derive from scouting ourselves, such a procedure suggests the added advantage of familiarizing the lower-level coaches with the varsity offense. We try to maintain offensive continuity among all levels of our program, but the individual preferences of the coaches can result in fairly significant differences by the end of the season. Alternating "home" scouting assignments among the coaches can help to avoid such a problem.

The *primary* purpose of scouting ourselves, however, is to find out what we're doing. If we identify our tendencies as our opponents do, we can predict with some success how they probably will defense us. Once we've made our predictions, we can start having more fun with misdirection. Figure 10-5 provides a sample page from a scouting report of one of our games. Because the opponent remained in a 5-2 defense throughout most of the game and chose to slash the defensive left end, we realized good success by running the power to the outside and having the lead blocker, the fullback, cut down the end.

As a complement to the play during this particular game, we called the power trap at four, especially as we observed the defensive tackle becoming "outside conscious" and the onside linebacker reacting hard to the outside on backfield action. It picked up fairly good yardage every time we called it, and it served to keep the defense honest the next time we ran the power to the outside.

Now assume that an upcoming opponent has determined that when we line up in a Pro 8 formation, we are likely to run to the right, probably with a power to the outside, maybe with a trap at four. Assume also that the opponent has determined that we tend to run *toward* our wingback; in essence that the wingback represents the probable direction of the play. In response to such an apparent tendency, a defensive coach can do any of several things to achieve a strategic edge. Certainly, he is unlikely to continue to play us straight up. He probably will try to

OFFENSIVE SCOUTING REPORT

Quarter _____ *1* _____

DOWN	YARD LINE	FORMATION	OPP. DEF.	PLAY	BALL CARR.	GAIN
1-10	D 32	Pro 8	52	P right	31	+ 4
2-6		Pro 8	52	P right	31	+4
3- 2		Pro 8	52	P trap 4	31	+6
4-						
1-10	D 46	T 8		X F8 action "Rt 8"	12/81	Inc.
2-10		T 8		1B pitch 8	31	+7
3-3		Wing 8		FB P right	36	+4
4-						
1-10	HP 43	T 7	52	Q 4	22	+5
2-5		T 7		X F 3	22	+2
3-3		Pro 8		P right	31	+ 7
4-						
1-10	HP 29	Pro 7	52	P left	22	+2
2-8		Pro 7		Q 3	36	+ 3
3-5		Pro 8		P right		+ 4
4-		Punt		—		
1-10	D 38	Pro 8	52	P right	31	+ 4
2-6		Pro 8		P tup 4		+5
3- 1		Pro 8		Q 3		+3
4-						

Figure 10-5

capitalize on the knowledge that he has gained from his scouting report. So will we.

A popular adjustment, especially with several of our opponents, is to slant the defensive line *away* from the wingback and to slide the linebackers *toward* the wingback. Such an adjustment will not constitute a steady diet for the defense, but it generally represents good strategy. Other adjustments might involve offsetting the noseman to his left, stacking the linebacker behind him, and "dealing" with them. Other adjustments could involve scraping the linebackers with the noseman or the defensive tackles, flexing the tackles with or without the scrape, or going into a totally different defense on first down, the time when we seemed most inclined to run the power to the outside.

Any combination of these or other defensive adjustments is possible. In addition, the defense is likely to be instructed to watch its keys carefully. For example, when the offense successfully has been running a power to the outside, the offside safety is likely to be told to watch the left halfback very carefully. Similarly, the fullback is the perfect key for the onside safety. Each of these keys is sure to bring the safeties to the point of attack, unless the offensive team has been scouting itself and is prepared to counter its previous tendencies.

And "counter" may be exactly the right word. Let's assume that early in the game we show a couple of "Pro 8/ Power right's" and that we observe the defensive line slanting hard away from the wingback. We also observe that the linebackers are compensating by sliding *toward* the wingback. In addition, the secondary is rotating on backfield action. Figure 10-6, a "Power counter at 5," does everything we want misdirection to do. It simulates the basic play; it is consistent with our past tendencies; and it keeps the defense honest, perhaps causes them to question their line stunts, certainly makes them less anxious to pursue on backfield action.

Consider another strategy. Assume that the defensive line is slanting away from the wingback as in the previous example or that the noseman and the offside linebacker are

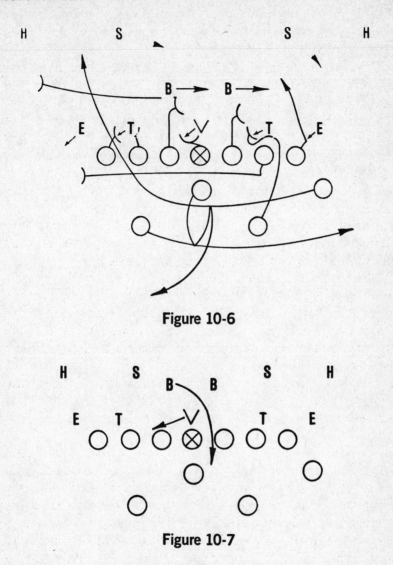

Figure 10-6

Figure 10-7

scraping as in Figure 10-7. Such a strategy certainly is reasonable. At least during this particular game, whenever we lined up in a Pro 8, we tended to run a power to the outside, a power trap at four, or a quick at three. The noseman's attempt to jam the one and three holes is a good way to shut down the quick at three and to knock the left guard off his path if the play is a trap at four or even a power to the outside. In like manner, the linebacker's attempt to blitz between the center and the right guard is a good way to jam the trap at four or to catch the left halfback as he runs the power to the outside. Each of these defensive maneuvers is fairly standard, primarily because they work, especially if the defense can predict what the offense is likely to do.

The counter already has been discussed as a good "tendency breaker," and it works just as well against scraping linebackers. So does the "Power slant trap at 1" from the Pro 8 formation. A quick-hitting misdirection play, the power slant trap, as diagrammed in Figure 10-8, provides the same advantages as the counter play. It keeps the defense honest and provides the strategy and the blocking patterns necessary to offset any adjustments made by the defense. For example, the double-team block will neutralize the noseman; and the left tackle, because the onside linebacker is likely to "scrape" himself out of the play, will be able to block the offside safety, who may try to follow the fullback to the point of attack. The onside safety probably will run

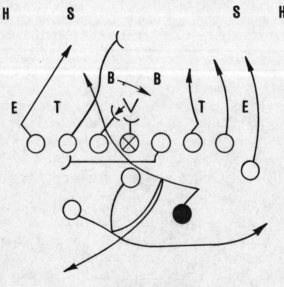

Figure 10-8

himself out of the play because of his key on the left halfback. Even if any of these players "senses" something wrong, the power slant trap hits so quickly that it is certain to pick up good yardage. And once it does, it reestablishes everything else we do.

Let's Wrap It Up

A bonus to be gained from this chapter is our method of calling formations. While it has simplified matters for us, it has complicated them for our opponents. We are able during any given game to run from as many as two to three hundred different formations. If we have developed a good idea of our tendencies, having scouted ourselves already, and the season is pointing toward an upcoming championship game, we can cause our final opponent a lot of trouble. Obviously, he will be *most* interested in what we do during the game just before his. That's a good time to use thirty different formations! Let him try to determine tendency by formation! Eventually he is likely to develop a pretty good idea of what we are doing, but it will have taken him a lot of valuable time, time which otherwise might have been spent refining his offense.

The real meat of the chapter, however, deals with scouting. The well-coordinated sideline staff is likely to identify weaknesses in almost any opposing defense and to suggest ways to attack those weaknesses. Obviously, much of this can be done, and is done, without the aid of scouting reports. Half-time and sideline adjustments will always be necessary But in the interests of good planning, offensively *and* defensively, it's always a good idea to know what the other guy is doing or is likely to do. Such knowledge gives you time to develop and to time new plays or to modify a few "old reliables." It's always a good idea to know what *you're* doing offensively—for much the same reason.

Misdirection is designed to enhance a team's unpredictability. It may do the opposite if a coach has fallen into a predictable pattern of integrating misdirection into his sequencing of plays. This can be done in several ways. The

coach may always set up a counter with one particular play
from one particular formation. He may tend to call a certain
counter play from a particular position on the field, from one
of the hash marks or from within the opposing team's ten
yard line, for example. He may always split an end when he
calls the "Crossfire 12 trap." Whatever his tendencies, sooner
or later someone is going to pick them up, and that someone
is likely to be his toughest rival.

Once this happens, he's "had," and he probably will not
know why or how. So we always scout ourselves, either by
having a lower-level assistant chart our calls or by breaking
down the films according to tendencies by formation, down
and distance, and field position. Reviewing the films probably is the most exact way to determine our tendencies,
because we can take the time to watch each play as often as
needed. But the scouting format we have developed is so
precise and involves such a minimum of writing that we
prefer to have a lower-level coach scout us on game days. On
such a basis, he is better able to get a "feel" for the game and
to make recommendations regarding player performance
and half-time adjustments. He also gains the advantage of
learning our offense and the philosophy that guides its use.
Then, when we review the films at a later time, we can use
his report as a guide to anticipate the films and to concentrate on the evaluation of the team's performance.

With his report in hand, we can get into our pre-game
planning much more quickly and then start to discuss the
strategies needed to break our tendencies while we attack
the opponent's. Obviously, misdirection is not the only way
to break offensive tendencies. If the opponent over-defends to
the side of the wingback, the offense can run or pass back to
the weak side of the formation. A "Pro 7/Fullback power
right," for example, is a good play if the line is slanting *away*
from the wingback and the linebackers are scraping or
sliding *toward* the wingback.

As evidenced in Figure 10-9, the fullback power away
from the wingback is a great "tendency breaker" to use
against the defense that established its adjustments based
upon your previous tendencies. It "two teams" the defensive

tackle and "kicks out" the defensive end. The hole is likely to
be big, especially if the linebackers are scraping. Obviously,
many other plays are available to the coach who wants to
break his tendencies. Misdirection as well as basic plays can
be very effective, depending upon the circumstances of the
game. The important point, however, is that all of us need to
take a close look at what we're doing offensively, as the old
Scottish poet, Bobby Burns, said: "…to see oursels as ithers
see us." And if you are the first of the "ithers," you will always
remain a couple of steps ahead of even your shrewdest
opponents.

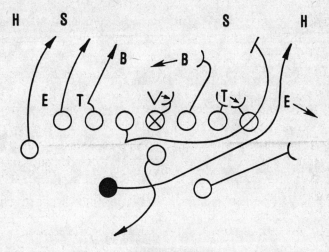

Figure 10-9

11

Practicing Misdirection

Sometimes practice can really be a drag—for players *and* coaches. And sometimes even the most inventive coach finds himself unable to do anything about it. No team can avoid the constant repetition of drills that are necessary to refine the timing and the basic techniques of a successful offense. Even blocking and running technique require almost daily practice. Most football players have an amazing facility to develop bad habits. The natural runner for example, with good kinesthetic sense, still may run straight up and may need to lower his shoulder when he hits the line. The runner's need for drill in fundamentals is less evident than a blocker's need to practice. Most bad habits creep in daily, especially when players get tired. Usually unconsciously, they look for the easy way out. Because of this, constant repetition of good habits is essential, especially for blockers. Most good runners are gifts from God; most good blockers are the creations of hard-working and knowledgeable football coaches.

Runners and blockers alike, however, require equal involvement in the timing of the offense. So what does the good coach do to relieve the tedium of timing drills? The answer, very simply, is darned little. Early in the season, while he describes the "big picture" for his players, he explains the need for timing and the personal commitment required for everyone to make it effective. Then he indicates that as the season progresses, no drill, other than live or dummy scrimmaging, will be any longer than fifteen or twenty minutes. He realizes that a tired or a bored football player develops bad habits, so he will develop a daily practice schedule that provides for several different drills.

While a fullback at the University of Nebraska, I learned several valuable lessons from the legendary Bob Devaney. One of the most important was that a fifteen to twenty minute drill encouraged maximum effort in me. I came to realize that when he called for a fifteen minute drill, it would be no longer than fifteen minutes. I also realized that if we did not execute correctly during that time, we would have another fifteen minutes on the following day. These two factors, then, the brevity of drill time and the inevitability of more drill time if we executed poorly, caused us to "put out" during each practice session.

The principle seemed to make sense then, and I have found that it makes sense now. It works equally well for college as well as for high school players. Be assured that at times the coaches leave certain drills thoroughly frustrated and praying for another half hour to get a few points across. But we soon realize that we can get to it tomorrow and that the benefits to be gained in player morale and effort far outweigh our momentary needs to work miracles.

The trick, then, if we can call it a trick, is to emphasize split-second timing by constantly repeating fundamentals and offensive execution ... but within spaces of time that allow coaches to make important comments and that encourage players to maximize their efforts. While all this is happening, coaches should be watching for key elements in execution. An often repeated mistake may require more than immediate correction; it may warrant another fifteen minute drill on the following day.

Keys to Success During Practice

Misdirection is exact. Basic plays require precision, but misdirection requires even more. If we are "to pull off the scam," misdirection must be executed so quickly that no one on the defense sees it. Certainly, such a goal is asking a great deal of high school football players, but the closer a team comes to such perfection, the more successful they will be. And the coach can help, first, by assuring a well-coordinated sideline staff and good strategic "know how" and, second, by knowing what to look for during practice.

The Big Picture

After the basic series have been introduced and practiced, the coach should introduce the misdirection plays, one at a time, and explain their complementary relationship with the basic series. Each player should have a general idea of what every other player is doing and of why he is doing it. Each does not necessarily need to know the actual assignments of the others, but a general understanding of the design and the purpose of each play is helpful if players are to execute their assignments properly. The fullback cannot run the 12 trap, for example, if he fails to read the left guard's block, nor can the left halfback lure the onside safety away from the five hole on a counter play if he does not execute a good fake.

This latter example illustrates a very important element in the execution of any misdirection play. Our emphases as high school coaches seem always to focus on running, blocking, and tackling. And why not? These three elements *define* football. But sometimes, especially after we have done a good job refining these skills in our players, we continue to emphasize them because we enjoy seeing a good thing done well—over and over again. It makes us feel good. But unfortunately, all this "feeling good" sometimes interferes with our need to emphasize the need for good faking. We forget at times that a good fake can accomplish as much as two or three good blocks. A defensive player who is out of position is as good as blocked, maybe even better. He's not even in the way.

So when we introduce the basic series, we emphasize faking just as much as we emphasize all the other fundamentals. It's a necessary part of the "big picture." Consider the "Inside belly counter at 5," as illustrated in Figure 11-1. We wouldn't want to run the play unless we had realized some previous success with the fullback running the belly at three or four. And we probably would have wanted at least *some* yardage with the inside belly option to the outside. When finally we run the counter play away from the basic action, therefore, the fullback had better do his job at four before the quarterback makes the handoff to the wingback, and the quarterback and the left halfback better do their jobs to the outside *after* the handoff. A good, extended fake from the quarterback after the handoff not only can influence the onside safety but can also cut down on the pursuit from the offside safety as well. It will also hold the offside linebacker after he realizes that the fullback does not have the ball. Faking, therefore, is very important.

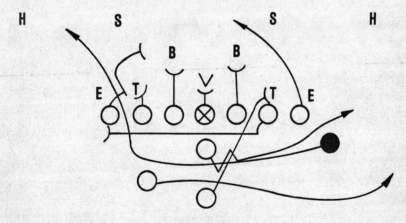

Figure 11-1

And it has to start from day *one*. How many times have all of us introduced plays and, especially early in the season, watched backs only to be sure that each was on the proper path or that players were in the right places at the right times. Certainly, we have all done this, and most of us have been guilty of not watching the fakes. We have been too pleased that the ball carrier got the handoff and entered the right hole at the right time.

No one can overemphasize the importance of proper timing and execution, but we accomplish it at times at the expense of other, equally important elements in the play. While we watch backfield paths and handoff fundamentals, players develop bad habits. Their fakes become perfunctory—routine—something that is done to kill time and eventually may even be forgotten, especially in the heat of battle when everyone becomes interested in how the ball carrier is doing. So coaches, too, after introducing the big picture, must keep the big picture in mind to assure that every player is doing what he is supposed to be doing during *every* play. By so doing we avoid all those costly bad habits that players can develop early in the season and that we may never break, no matter how hard we try later.

Watch the Loafers

This latter point suggests another. Almost every team has one or more prima donnas who feel that practice is "uncool" and that game time is the only time to put out. Even though such players usually can pull it off individually, their effects on the collective efforts of the team can be devastating. If the timing of misdirection plays is to come close to any standard of perfection, *every* player, even the prima donnas, must execute the plays in practice exactly as they will be executed during a game. If a player is expected to go half to three-quarter speed, he must *practice* at half to three-quarter speed; if a player is expected to go full speed, he must *practice* at full speed. If only one player loafs through timing, the execution of the entire play will suffer.

The principle of fifteen to twenty minute drills as *maximum* times is very useful in the above circumstance. Even the most well-motivated and dedicated player will begin to "ease off" as the length of a timing drill grows longer and longer. For this reason it is unwise to organize a timing drill for the entire crossfire or inside belly series. The plays are too numerous. In their haste to get through the entire series, coaches may even slack off. They may disregard the mention of key points. Of equal importance, after the first fifteen to twenty minutes, the drill reaches a point of diminishing returns as players lose interest in what they are doing or as they lose sight of the purpose of the drill.

And kindergarten gimmicks to maintain motivation during lengthy drills have limited value. "Rewarding" players by giving them fewer sprints after practice may work once in a while, but even that loses its appeal when the drill begins to drag on. In addition, such a gimmick deprives the player of needed conditioning, something that just might help win a ball game late in the fourth quarter.

More Big Picture

Games are won late in the fourth quarter by the team that is well-conditioned and that keeps the big picture in focus. Another important element during any practice session, then, is to time all the plays, especially the misdirection plays, with an offensive line. Having a line in front of the backs conditions them to watch for trap and double team blocks and helps them to standardize their paths during any given play. Conversely, when the line is practicing its blocking assignments, it should have a backfield executing the plays. The line needs to know where the back is and when he is likely to hit the hole. The tackles on counter traps need constant reminders to move down the line of scrimmage as fast as they can, otherwise they will hold up the wingback, slowing the play and giving the defense valuable time to react to it. Nothing serves as a better reminder to the pulling tackle than the pitter patter of little feet behind him while he moves down the line of scrimmage to execute his trap block.

When the line practices its assignments, the backs need not be first stringers. The same is true of the linemen when the backfield is practicing timing. Third and fourth stringers or defensive specialists who have knowledge of the assignments can be used. The timing requirements of each play will be satisfied if someone can be available to complete the "big picture." This means that when the backs are timing their plays, the first and second string linemen can receive all the attention of the line coach while he puts them through their paces. Conversely, when the line is practicing its assignments, the backfield coach can devote most of his time to the first two teams as they practice blocking or running technique.

The Quarterback Is Focal

One final point involves specific reference to one player, the quarterback. Because he is focal within every play and because his timing is essential within every play, the quarterback requires close supervision early in the season, especially during the practice of misdirection plays. The quarterback's mistakes are magnified ten times over. A critical mistake from the quarterback has implications for every player on the field, so early in the season we watch him very closely.

A case in point involves counter plays, especially within the quick and inside belly series. The quarterbacks must learn, from the first day on, to watch the wingback early in the play. Because the handoff to the wingback must be quick and exact, the quarterback must "sense" the fullback or see him only peripherally during the initial part of the play. He must devote most of his attention to the wingback. This element within each of these plays should not be difficult for the quarterback to learn because he has the similar responsibility of watching the defensive end during the early part of the quick and the inside belly *options*.

The coach should watch the quarterback very carefully early in the season to be sure that he is *not* looking at the fullback during either the option or the counter play. When the plays are first introduced and practiced, the quarterback will want to watch the fullback, especially during the inside belly series. If he develops the bad habit of doing so, it will be very difficult to break, especially during games, when the pressure is on to execute a good fake. So the coach should watch the quarterback's eyes very carefully. If he fails to do so, and the quarterback persists in watching the fullback during the fake, he eventually will make a poor exchange with the wingback on the counter play. In addition, during the inside belly option to the outside, a hard-charging defensive end is likely to dismember him in front of a horrified crowd!

The First Few Days

During the first few days of practice in the fall, we introduce all the plays, one series per day, including the misdirection plays, by diagramming them on the board and by discussing the distinguishing characteristics and special requirements of each series. Following the large-group discussion, we put the line and the backs into separate classrooms and introduce the unique needs of each play within the series as it relates to their positions. Then we keep the line and the backs separated and take the field. The line goes over its blocking assignments, and the backs practice the timing of each play. In each instance the seniors are used, partly because they already are familiar with the timing of each play but primarily because they run each play to near perfection in their eagerness to impress all the juniors who are watching them.

We indicate to them before each series that we want the plays runs exactly as they were diagrammed and discussed in the classroom. And they usually do just that, sometimes to an extreme. But that is just what we want from them. It conditions the juniors, some of whom will be starters within a few weeks, to run the right paths and to extend the fakes well into the line.

Following this general introduction, we divide all the juniors into units, have them execute their assignments, and encourage them to ask questions. The key principle during this period of time is "Ask a question and be a dummy for ten seconds; don't ask it and be a dummy forever." By the end of the first week, much of which has been without pads, we usually have most of the offense introduced, as well as our system of calling offensive formations. The kids pick it up quickly. Of course, it does not hurt to have the same formation-calling system and fundamentally the same offense in operation at the lower levels.

By the time we inherit most of the varsity players, they are familiar with most of the offense. All that remains for us to do is to introduce the more sophisticated plays: a few of the counters, all of the slant traps, and the options. Obviously, most of the misdirection is new to them when they reach the varsity. They will have had some of it, but normally the freshman and sophomore coaches are too busy having players master the basic series and work on fundamentals to get into the precision of misdirection.

One final point regarding the first few days, and an important one, involves the relationship between juniors and seniors. Both realize from the first day of practice that every senior is going to get the *first* chance to make the team. Any junior who eventually plays is going to have to beat out every senior in that position, no matter how good we know the junior is. Walking into a first or a second string position during the first week does not help the junior, who does not learn how to scratch for his job. And it has a more serious effect on the seniors in that position, who may have been waiting for three years to get a chance at that starting position.

This principle of giving seniors the first shot, though fairly obvious, is extremely important. It accomplishes three things. One, it holds each senior and encourages his investment in the program. Two, it makes each junior work up to his potential. And, three, it avoids that junior-senior conflict that can hamper the team's success. Our juniors, no matter how successful at the sophomore level, know that they are *rookies* and will remain so until they prove something to us and to the seniors in their positions.

The Next Couple of Weeks

That's one reason why when we start scrimmaging we have the seniors running the offense and the juniors trying to stop them. The seniors find out how tough some of those juniors are, given their desire to impress us and to make the first two teams. And the juniors gain an almost immediate respect for the diversity of our offense. While two or three of them are unloading on our fullback at the four hole, our wingback is prancing through the five hole with one of our counter plays. The juniors become believers and listen carefully from that point on.

That's one reason why they learn very quickly. After a week or two, they learn to sense a counter play, not so much the slant traps, but they pick up the counter plays very well. This suggests one of the problems with some forms of misdirection. Sooner or later, our opponents, especially those who use counter plays, begin to sense them. That signals our need to introduce a little camouflage, in effect to re-introduce them to a little defensive honesty.

By this time, of course, most of the good juniors have found their spots on the first two or three teams. So the introduction of camouflage is used to keep the junior varsity players on the defense honest. It also can be a lot of fun, and it is certain to be used against the better teams as we get into the season

Misdirection as Camouflage

Figure 11-2 illustrates the "T 8/Inside belly option at 8/ Counter action." Once the defensive secondary and the defensive ends become conscious of the wingback's counter move, his use as a decoy is sometimes preferable to his blocking. His counter action fake accomplishes two things. One, it influences the end and secondary. It can draw them away from the point of attack or, more normally, can cause them to relax for a split second. By that time, the ball carrier is upon them, as in Figure 11-3, which is a "T 8/Crossfire 12 trap/ Counter action." The backfield action for this particular play would involve a hand fake to the left halfback, an almost simultaneous hand off to the fullback, and a follow-up fake to the wingback, who should give every appearance of running the ball at the five hole.

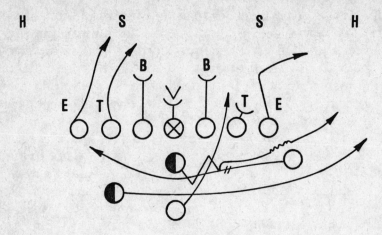

Figure 11-2

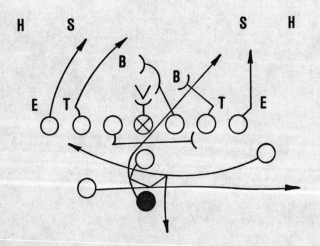

Figure 11-3

Two, the counter action fake, as in each of these examples, reminds the defense that the wingback's move down the
line of scrimmage does not necessarily mean that the offense
is running a counter play. We already have shown them that
the wingback's counter fake may be setting up a screen play
or a play-action pass. Now we let them know that it may be
camouflaging a running play as well. And we can run the
counter fake with most of our basic plays. By the time an

opponent has played us several times, he may develop a general "feel" for what we are likely to do, but he can never really be sure. Too much of what we do looks like everything else we do. This keeps them very honest.

Fun with Misdirection

By definition, misdirection is fun. It provides variety for the players and unpredictability for the fans. But sometimes it can get downright silly. Our sophomore head coach, a former fullback on one of Iowa's Rose Bowl teams, has pushed the reverse play about as far as it can be pushed. A couple of years ago, during one of his several championship seasons, he ran the ultimate reverse. The score was tied against one of his toughest opponents with about ten seconds remaining until halftime. He was on his own forty yard line and apparently decided that it was time for a little harmless fun, so he called his "Quinella." The name doesn't necessarily describe the number of reverses, but it comes close.

As diagrammed in Figure 11-4, the play starts off as a power right and ends up with the left guard running the ball around the right end. The sophomores have run it at least two times a season, but on this particular day, the left guard, later to become a middle linebacker on the varsity's state championship team, ran through the entire opposing team for a sixty-yard touchdown. The crowd buzzed for hours afterwards. And they never missed a loud roar of approval every time he ran it thereafter.

We, as yet, have not mustered up the courage to run it, probably because of all those handoffs, but it still serves to highlight a fundamental reality about the game of football. It ought to be fun. We can build character and help to sublimate adolescent tensions, but if we have fun while we're doing it, we'll do it just that much better.

But we have not handed the ball off to our guards or tackles *yet*. We have thrown two or three "tackle eligibles," but the tackles are not a part of the running game yet. They

already have enough to do. We have given the ball to our
ends, however. They enjoy the chance to run the ball out of
the backfield, and we have found that, on occasion, the "end
counter" can be very effective strategically.

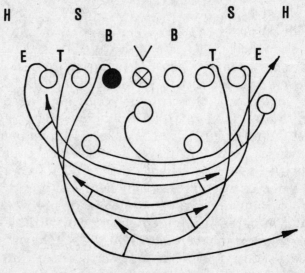

Figure 11-4

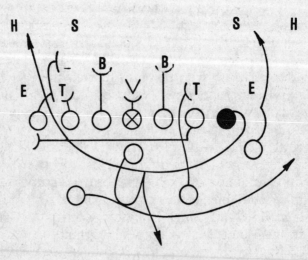

Figure 11-5

The "Pro 8/Power *end* counter at 5," as illustrated in Figure 11-5, gives us the counter play without the obvious wingback key. It has been quite successful for us the few times we have run it, and it has kept the ends smiling for days afterward. Obviously, it can be used with the counter plays from the other series as well. Its success, however, other than for fun, is normally limited by the running skills and the general maneuverability of our ends. They are usually built for blocking and catching, not for running. Even their acceptance of such limitations doesn't interfere with their desire to run the play, though. They love it—and it is fun to watch them.

Let's Wrap It Up

Several important points about practicing misdirection were discussed in this chapter. The most important point involved the need to organize frequent drills—in small doses, no longer than fifteen to twenty minutes each. Such a principle provides for frequent repetition of critical elements within each misdirection play and encourages the maximum effort of each player, even the prima donnas who are disinclined to "put out" during practice sessions. Obviously, the principle of frequent but abbreviated drills is appropriate for other plays within the offense and for the practice of fundamentals as well. The variety it provides keeps players enthusiastic throughout practice and prevents much of the "standing around" that characterizes certain drills. But it seems especially appropriate for the timing of misdirection plays because their needed precision requires frequent repetition.

Another important point that relates to the practice of misdirection is the need to integrate it within timing drills as well as scrimmage sessions. Counters and other misdirection plays should not be the exclusive focus of any one drill. Misdirection is not an entity unto itself. It is designed to complement the plays within a basic series. If the players practice the basic as well as the misdirection plays concurrently, they will be sure to realize the complementary nature of each and to run the plays accordingly.

This reality suggests the final important point to be made regarding the practice of misdirection. While important within most of the basic plays, faking is particularly important within the misdirection plays. The execution of each play is not correct until every fake has been extended well into the line and run at full speed. Each back must regard faking as being as important as running or blocking. Faking may not involve the same kind of crowd recognition, but it can get the backfield coach awfully excited. And, when all is said and done, he is for the backs the source from which all blessings flow—or at least he should be.

If the game of football is *really* like the game of life, then every player should realize that some things aren't always fun; they are simply necessary. Practice is one of them. The old saying indicates that practice makes perfect; no one said that it makes entertainment. But it can provide an enormous amount of fun on game days when the offense takes the field and clicks off its plays to near perfection. Players must realize, fortunately most of them do, that practice is a necessary element in the day-to-day preparation of a well-oiled football machine. Coaches can help, too, by realizing that frequent but abbreviated drills keep the purpose of the drill in focus and help to maintain the attention and to maximize the efforts of the players.

Figure 11-6 illustrates a sample page from one of our practices. It reveals a variety of activities, most of which are fifteen minutes in length and all of which encourage the maximal efforts of players. That is all that is really required if a team is to perfect its fundamental skills and its strategic effectiveness. Players must learn, through the mature direction of their coaches, that football involves work as well as play, sacrifice as well as reward, and team commitment as well as individual recognition. With these thoughts in mind, most players will accept practice as the opportunity to perfect their skills and to contribute to the ultimate success of their team.

DAILY PRACTICE PLAN   DATE *Sept. year*

	ACTIVITY	EQUIPMENT	REMARKS
1. *2:10* to *2:25*			
GUARDS			
TACKLES	*Blocking*	*14*	
CENTERS	*assignments*	*stand ups*	
ENDS			
OBS	*XF Series*		
BACKS	*timing*		
2. *2:25* to *2:40*			
GUARDS			
TACKLES	*Pass blocking*		
CENTERS			
ENDS	*Play-action*	*7 air flates*	*semi-live pass*
OBS	*screens*		*rush*
BACKS			
3. *2:40* to *2:55*			
GUARDS			
TACKLES	*Blocking*		
CENTERS	*fundamentals*		
ENDS			
OBS	*Passing techique*		
BACKS	*Blocking*	*4 stand ups*	
4. *2:55* to *3:10*			
GUARDS			
TACKLES			*Emphasize*
CENTERS	*Half line*		*double-team and*
ENDS	*scrimmage /*		*fullback blocks*
OBS	*Powers right*		
BACKS	*and left*		

Figure 11-6

12

Misdirection in the Major Universities

Misdirection is a relatively new term, but the plays that it suggests are as old as football itself. Crossbucks, counters, slant traps, and bootlegs are but a few of the ways that teams have used misdirection. The good teams, such as Michigan, Nebraska, and Oklahoma, integrate misdirection into their offenses so that it complements their basic series and becomes an essential part of their strategy. They use misdirection both as a weapon to gain needed yardage and as a ploy to confuse defensive keys. Misdirection for them is a part of their attack, an important element which complements the offense and makes it collectively more potent than the sum of its individual parts. A team's basic series, which for some high school football teams may constitute their entire offense, can be very effective, if the team is well-prepared for its opponents and well-coached fundamentally.

Conversely, misdirection, used extensively by many teams, offers excitement to the fans and suggests an unpredictable dimension for the running offense. But when basic plays *and* misdirection plays are combined and are well-coordinated within the offense, the cumulative effect is greater than the sum of the two parts. The running offense becomes a surprisingly potent weapon. Certainly, good football teams are aware of such synergistic effects of misdirection. That's why they use it so extensively and why each realizes such success

The Big Guys

Coach "Bo" Schembechler has one of the best collegiate records in the country. During his career, Schembechler's teams have compiled a record of 154-38-6 and have accepted several bowl bids. Coach Barry Switzer's eight year record at the University of Oklahoma is 83-9-2; and Coach Tom Osborne at the University of Nebraska has established a record of 75-20-2. Each of the coaches has earned a national reputation for his knowledge of the game as well as for his dynamic leadership and personal contribution to the success and excitement of intercollegiate football.

Because their offenses are different in design, we have decided to use them as examples of the wide application of misdirection. Each of the three coaches was contacted personally and asked to complete a short questionnaire that characterized his use of misdirection. In addition, each coach was asked to offer one or more explanatory comments and to suggest basic principles which direct his team's use of misdirection. Each was not asked to provide specific examples of successful plays but to indicate only generally the kinds of plays which have worked best for them.

The following sections, therefore, will identify the coaches' principles and will provide examples of plays which reflect them. Our purpose is not to reveal the intricacies of the plays which have contributed to each team's success but to provide examples of the principles which each coach has identified as important. As we consider each team's use of misdirection, keep in mind that any creative coach, familiar with the principles of misdirection, can design specific plays which complement his offense and capitalize on the unique strengths of his athletes. The following plays, however, have been "field tested" for years—and they work.

The University of Michigan

"Charisma" is a much over-used term. But, as over-used as it may be, it seems to be the only way to describe "Bo" Schembechler. Coach Schembechler is a gum-chewing, energetic, and outspoken master of the game of football. He has established a national reputation not only for his personal courage but for his exceptional leadership at the University of Michigan.

Coach Schembechler uses a variety of misdirection plays. He indicates that slant traps, reverses, counter plays from the "home" position, crossbucks, and bootlegs are used regularly within his offense. But he emphasizes that slant traps and bootlegs have been most successful for him. He also makes exceptional use of the crossbuck.

Coach Schembechler uses it as well as anyone in football. He indicates that the trap option is his best misdirection play, and, considering how he uses it, its success is not surprising. Variously called the trap option, the crossfire option, or the buck option, the play epitomizes the complementary relationships among basic plays, misdirection, and play-action passing.

Although run from the same backfield action, the trap option can become a fullback trap, a quarterback trap, an option to the outside, or a pass. It has all the characteristics of an effective as well as an exciting series.

Figure 12-1 illustrates an "I 10/Crossfire trap at 1/Option action." This is not Michigan's terminology, but it's very close to the play they run, and as such it provides an excellent example of Michigan's principle of "Keep 'em guessing." The play can be very effective, especially if the quarterback and the tailback execute good fakes to the outside after the ball is handed to the fullback. Without good fakes, the play becomes just another fullback trap, and its relationship to other plays within the series is lost.

As one of my old coaches used to say, "Run your fullback. If you want a successful offense, run your fullback." Michigan's buck or trap option, as diagrammed in Figure 12-2, illustrates this principle well. Once the team realizes

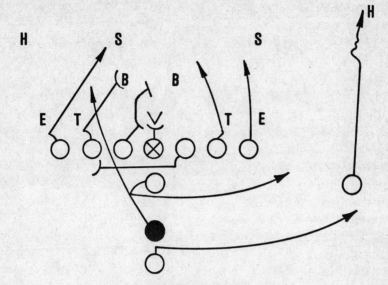

Figure 12-1

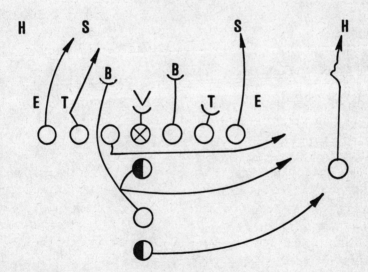

Figure 12-2

success with the fullback trap, the "I 10/Trap option at 8" becomes the perfect complement. Because the linebackers are likely to be influenced by the fullback's fake, the quarterback can option the defensive end to get to the outside. In addition, on the option play, they lead with the "guard off," a strategy which further complicates the defense's dilemma. It does so, first, by providing a lead blocker for the quarterback and, second, by adding yet another dimension to the sequencing of the play.

This added dimension, as illustrated in Figure 12-3 becomes a problem not only for the defensive tackle but also for the secondary, none of whom can be absolutely certain where the point of attack is. Now, instead of leading the quarterback to the outside on the option play, the left guard *traps* the defensive tackle and the quarterback runs the ball behind him. If *anyone* on the defense is over-pursuing, the linebackers and the safeties in particular, the opposing team can be in real trouble. The quarterback will simply cut behind the guard's trap block and find the open spaces up the middle.

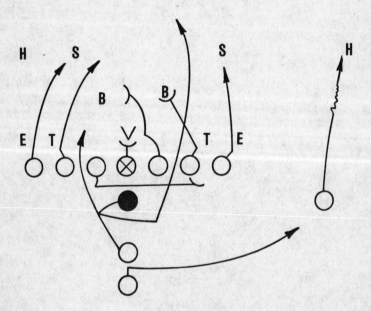

Figure 12-3

Finally, imagine the safety's predicament as he watches the quarterback following the guard down the line of scrimmage. Not only must he decide where the play will hit but he also has to contend with the tight end, who can confuse the issue even more by transforming an apparent blocking attempt into a pass route. The tight end will stalk the safety, as illustrated in Figure 12-4, and, when the safety reacts to him, will release into his pass route, a quick flag. The quarterback gives every appearance of running the option play to the outside, then, after four or five steps down the line of scrimmage, makes his drop and looks for the tight end somewhere underneath the flankerback's deep move. Even if he is not open, the tailback is an excellent choice out in the flat.

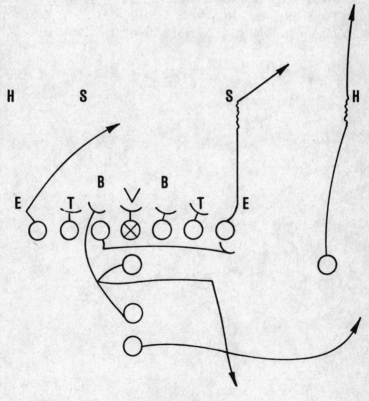

Figure 12-4

The plays within the series, as illustrated in figures 12-1 through 12-4, are so well sequenced that the defense can never really trust their keys, nor can they be sure if the play is a pass or a run, often until it is too late. As with all good misdirection plays, this particular sequence is especially unpredictable and provides but one indication of why Michigan has been so successful.

Coach Schembechler also indicated that crossing patterns with action away are very successful pass plays for Michigan. Figure 12-5 diagrams an "I 10/Crossfire bootleg pass at 7," which illustrates an example of Schembechler's comment. It starts from the same offensive set as his trap option and from fundamentally the same backfield action. Even if run with limited success, the bootleg tendency away from backfield action prevents the opposing team from overloading the defense to the side of the flanker.

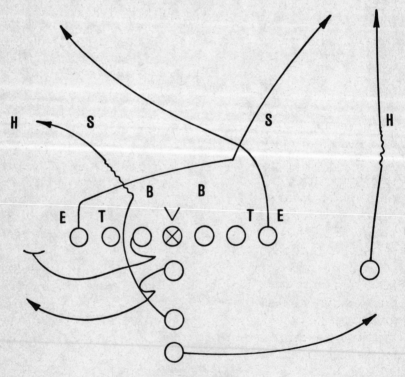

Figure 12-5

But this play rarely is run with limited success. The backfield action combined with the left end's slant move across the middle tends to influence the onside safety away from the area of the intended pass. Even if out of position only a few steps, he still has a tough time recovering to help the right halfback, who has two men in his zone. Usually, one of the linebackers has the responsibility of covering the fullback. The linebackers are likely to be too preoccupied by the backfield action to be concerned with the fullback, especially if he becomes a good "deceiver" and *sneaks* into the secondary.

It is important that the left end run a shallow slant move during the first half of his pattern, then break diagonally toward the flag in order to force the coverage of the offside safety. The shallow first half of the pattern should hold the onside safety, encourage him to think run, and have him out of position by the time the right end enters his zone. Ideally, the right end should be able to get behind the onside safety and be in a position to make the reception in the deep part of the safety's zone. If he does not receive the ball, he should be in a position to block for the fullback who will make his reception somewhere underneath.

The characteristics of bootleg passes already described apply to this play as well. The fullback must be careful to slow up the penetration of anyone on the line of scrimmage. The quarterback must take his time with the fakes in order to hold the defense, maybe even to encourage the secondary's rotation on backfield action. He also must be conscious of the run possibility, even if the play was called a pass in the huddle. This, however, will be determined by his awareness of down and distance.

Again, these plays may not be exactly the plays that Michigan runs, but they are darned close. The important point is that we can learn something from one of the game's great coaches. Misdirection, even within option plays, adds that critical dimension of unpredictability that keeps defenses guessing. It works for Michigan. That says it all.

The University of Nebraska

Tom Osborne was one of my coaches at the University of Nebraska. He is a most impressive man, youthful, soft-spoken, very intelligent, and dedicated to his athletes and to the game of football. Since taking the reins from Coach Bob Devaney a few years ago, Coach Osborne has compiled an impressive record and has maintained Nebraska's well-earned reputation for exciting and hard-nosed football.

Nebraska can run from several backfield sets, but within the past few years they have emphasized the Double Wing and the I Wing. From these formations, Coach Osborne indicates that they run reverses, bootlegs, and counter plays, the counter play from the wing position being one of their most successful plays. As a matter of fact, Nebraska runs so many wingback counters and passes the ball so well that Coach Osborne indicated, "We have often had our best athlete at wingback."

Considering the crop of talented athletes playing for Nebraska, that is some statement. And it serves to emphasize the importance of the wingback, a point that has been made several times throughout this book. A good wingback is a constant threat to the defensive secondary, no matter what he does. Even disregarding blocking skills, his skills as a runner and a pass receiver make him a very dangerous person.

Particularly dangerous is his ability to run the counter. Most teams that run from the "I" formation execute a lot of power plays, usually off tackle. Nebraska is no exception. Within the past several years, they have been blessed with several exceptionally gifted tailbacks. In addition, their backfield coach can teach blocking as well as anyone in the country. The power play, then, is a natural. And Nebraska has gotten a lot of yardage with it; *mileage* may be a better word. They normally are among the top five teams in the country in total offense.

An excellent play to complement the power from the I formation is the "I 8/Power counter at 5," illustrated in Figure 12-6. The power play, if run effectively, attracts the

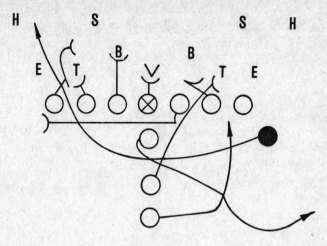

Figure 12-6

attention of the linebackers and both safeties, especially if it is run up the middle as well as off tackle. The counter play, then, becomes an excellent key breaker and, as usual, a good way to keep the defense honest. The power counter can be run several different ways, but two variations are especially effective from the I formation.

Figure 12-6 illustrates the first. Many teams, Nebraska included, position the tailback deep in the backfield, up to six yards, maybe more. The idea is to let him run to daylight, to give him time to read the defensive stunts and to adjust to them. The idea has merit, and it also provides for a particularly deceptive counter play. With the tailback so deep, the wingback can come immediately, right after the fullback clears, to take an outside hand off from the quarterback. Immediately after the hand off, the quarterback moves to the tailback, fakes to him, and then drops as if to pass the ball. All that is required to help with the timing is a split-second delay from both the quarterback and the tailback immediately after the ball is snapped, not so long as to provide a key to the defense, but long enough to give the wingback time to beat the tailback to the point of exchange.

It's a good play. The hand off is shielded, and the subsequent fake helps to attract even more attention from the secondary. Another variation involves the way we run it,

as illustrated in Figure 12-7. Because we commit our tailback
to a particular hole, we want to hit the point of attack as fast
as possible, so we line him up a maximum of five yards
behind the quarterback. Such positioning requires the quarterback to execute an *inside* hand off *after* he fakes to the
tailback on the power action. We instruct him to reverse
open, to mesh with the tailback and ride him momentarily,
then to hand to the wingback. After the hand off, he drops as
if to pass the ball.

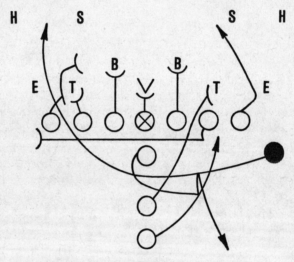

Figure 12-7

Regardless of which play a team runs, the counter play
can do much not only to keep the defense honest but also to
pick up valuable yardage. The University of Nebraska has
proved consistently that wingback counters are important
plays within any offense and that the wingback is one of the
team's most important players.

The University of Oklahoma

Although triple option teams seem to run either the
fullback or the option most of the time, the counter is one of
their best plays. Coach Barry Switzer has created a football

machine at the University of Oklahoma. Traditionally a national football power, Oklahoma has lost only nine games within the past eight years; and, during much of that time, they have used the triple option. They have used it with such success and Coach Switzer has so dominated the sport that even the native Oklahomans, the diehards most proud of Oklahoma soil, have seriously considered renaming the state "Switzer" land. Their keen desire for originality probably is the only thing preventing them from doing so.

Coach Switzer indicates that Oklahoma uses reverses, ends around, and counter plays from the "home" position as their chief forms of misdirection. As with most wishbone teams, his most successful misdirection play is the counter from the home position. As Coach Switzer indicates, "The Wishbone creates pursuit problems for the defense, and counters are always good versus running defenses."

Defenses have enough problems stopping the "Bone," even without an effective counter play. But when the offense adds plays such as the counter dive and the counter dive option, the defense is in bigger trouble. The "Wishbone/Counter dive," as diagrammed in Figure 12-8, compounds the defense's problems with their keys.

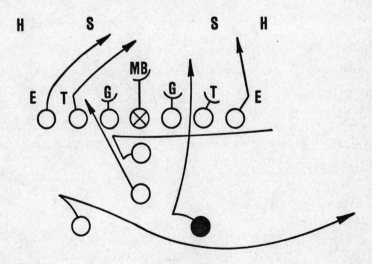

Figure 12-8

Consider the 6-1 or the 4-3 defense. Most teams will have the middle linebacker key the fullback, and the safeties key the home halfbacks. Other variations are possible, but these keys tend to be standard. Middle linebackers also tend to be very conscious of the quarterback's opening move. Because the quarterback is opening, and fullback is running away from the point of attack, the middle linebacker is unable to help when the right halfback dives into the four hole. If the offensive right end executes a good fake on the onside safety, the play can get a lot of yardage.

Its complement, the "Wishbone/Counter dive option at 8," illustrated in Figure 12-9, can cause even more problems. The fullback's move away from the point of attack virtually eliminates the middle linebacker. The onside safety, once he reacts to the right halfback's dive fake, is of no help to the outside. The defensive end will have a decision to make between the quarterback and the pitchback, but he is likely to be assigned the pitchback. And the defensive halfback probably will be assigned an outside-in pursuit path because he has to represent the last line of defense to the outside. In addition, the halfback will be avoiding the right end's block.

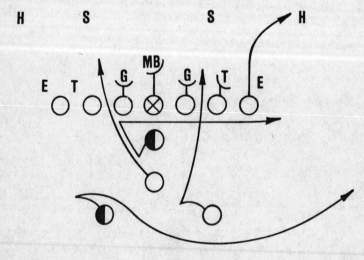

Figure 12-9

All of this is why wishbone quarterbacks pick up so much yardage. Who's left to cover him? Unfortunately for the wishbone teams, they are unable to predict this kind of coverage all the time. If they could, there would be no stopping them. Most defenses will vary the assignments of their personnel in order to confuse the blocking assignments and the sequencing of the offense.

But the fact remains, a good wishbone team, certainly one like Oklahoma, is going to pick up a lot of yardage, much of it with their quarterback. And while they are doing it, everyone on the defense seems to be helpless to do anything about it! There's nothing like watching Oklahoma on television, especially with one of my enthusiastic but rather uninformed friends I recall one literally screaming at a defensive end who seemed to be running *away* from the ball carrier, the quarterback on an option play, one similar to the play illustrated earlier. After providing a brief but detailed explanation of the defensive end's responsibility for the pitchback, my friend exclaimed, "Well, then, who the heck has the quarterback?!."

The ultimate question.

If Oklahoma's opponents could answer that one with any degree of consistency, they probably would be able to salvage their psyches and retain some of their pride

Let's Wrap It Up

The comments of these three coaches serve as an excellent summary for the topic of misdirection. The fact that they use misdirection is no suprise. Its contributions to game strategy are significant, primarily because of the unpredictability it suggests In order to use it effectively, however, coaches must remember a few important principles guiding its use.

1. Misdirection is not an entity unto itself. Misdirection, like play-action passes, cannot exist without a foundation of basic plays. It consists of plays that complement the basic series within an offense. This fact suggests two important considerations. One, when each play is introduced to the team, the coach should emphasize the "big picture." Every player should understand the fundamental relationship between basic and misdirection plays. Two, basic and misdirection plays should be run alternately during timing drills and scrimmage sessions to underscore that basic relationship. If players understand how misdirection relates to the basic plays, they will be more convincing when they run them and will give each the "sell job" that it requires to be successful.

2. Misdirection does not have to be fancy to be successful. The plays which illustrated the misdirection used by some of the most successful college teams in the country were simple in design and involved but one hand off. Anything more complicated than those discussed in this book can be confusing to the players and can increase the risk of mistake. Multiple hand offs and elaborate backfield action do little more than take time to execute. They may look good on paper or even during a dummy scrimmage, but they won't get the job done on game days.

3. Even though it is basically simple, misdirection requires timing. The plays are not as intricate as they are precise. The ball cannot be seen between fake and hand off. To look like a basic play, a counter, slant trap, or crossbuck requires exact timing and should be rehearsed almost daily, but in drill sessions short enough to sustain the interest and energy levels of the players and to maintain focus on the purpose of the drill.

4. Put a good athlete at wingback, maybe your best, if you plan to run wingback counters. Even when not running the ball (and he must be an excellent runner), he will be either receiving a pass or making a key block. The University of Nebraska, along with several other major universities, often has its best athlete at wingback—and not without good reason. Even when not directly involved in the execution of the play, the wingback, if well-respected by the defense, can be an excellent decoy to draw attention away from the point of attack. His primary strengths, however, are his football skills. You may have better blockers, better pass receivers, and better runners on your team, but no one should be able to combine all three better than your wingback.

5. Use misdirection unpredictably. Two words characterize misdirection best: complementarity and unpredictability. The first word, complementarity, has been discussed extensively already. So has unpredictability, but a few more words are necessary if a team is to make the best possible use of misdirection. Scouting your opponents is important if you are to design the best possible combinations of plays for each game. So is scouting yourself. In addition to the possibility of having developed several obvious tendencies with your basic offense, you may be using your misdirection plays predictably. A simple but thorough scouting format will enable you to look at yourself as well as your opponent. What you learn about yourself may surprise you into doing things a little differently.

6. Establish good sideline procedure. The knowledge of what your opponent is doing *while* you are playing him is often more important than the information you get *before* you play him. Such knowledge is needed not only to make sideline or halftime adjustments in game strategy but also to identify the proper sequence for plays.

If the inside belly at four is picking up yardage, good football strategy would dictate that you "keep going to the well." But if the inside belly at four gets shut down by a slashing defensive tackle, you might want to finesse him and run the left halfback with the inside belly at six. But you might never know that the tackle is slashing. So, in order to make the adjustment or to determine the right sequence, someone on the sidelines or in the press box will have to watch each play and provide you with the information needed to help call the next play. This may seem quite fundamental to some coaches, but many of us need a reminder or two to get it done systematically.

7. Coordinate the entire offense by using play-action passes. Misdirection complements the basic series, and play-action passing complements them both. Coach Schembechler's trap option series at the University of Michigan is the perfect example of how the same backfield action can become a quarterback trap, a trap option to the outside, or a play-action pass to the tight end. The defense is forced to play a guessing game, something they would rather not do. Play-action provides such a dimension for the high school coach. As indicated in an earlier chapter, it equalizes the advantage that the defense has in simple fundamentals and gives the strategic edge to the offense. For most high schools, it represents the only way to throw, not only because it uses the quarterback's talents more effectively but also because it does so much to help the running game.

Perhaps the best way to conclude a book on misdirection is with a quote from Barry Switzer, Oklahoma's head coach. In response to my request for additional information, he concluded his questionnaire with the comment, "Good players make good plays." I doubt that such a quote will ever be etched in stone, but it does make good sense. Perhaps that's one reason why many college campuses witness an exodus of coaches each winter and spring in search of the "Blue Chipper." It sounds somewhat like a hunting expedition—only because it is. The school that "bags" the most blue chippers increases its chances of avoiding famine for another few years. The "hunting" the coaches find themselves involved in, then, is not so much for sport as it is for survival.

Not so suprisingly, the schools that get the blue chippers also seem to hire blue chip coaches. The end result is a football program that develops the habit of winning and is able to attribute much of its success to its athletes—as Coach Switzer does. Colleges, then, are not so much blessed with good athletes as they are familiar with the ways to get them.

If a *high school* coach gets a blue chipper, he is blessed with him, more like a thankful parent than a skillful hunter. For the high school coach, the blue chipper is hardly recognizable in his infancy but becomes a big bundle of joy from heaven. Along with this sudden "parenthood," however, goes the responsibility of assuring his growth. When the young player is first introduced to high school football, he is unfamiliar with even the most basic fundamentals. By the time he completes his high school career, the young athlete, always with his coach's assistance and concern, has matured into a talented and experienced football player—sometimes into a blue chipper.

So the high school coach has a responsibility that is really quite different from the college coach. His responsibility seems more significant, if less celebrated. Like a parent, he must protect his boy from developing bad habits; he must provide him an understanding of the football world; he must help him explore the values that realize humility in victory and resolution in defeat; he must instill in his boy a commitment to the team as well as an investment in his own growth; and he must assure his boy's love of the game and respect for his opponents.

These are important considerations. If they are not developed in each athlete before he graduates from high school, he is unlikely to develop them in college. It seems, then, that college coaches *recruit* blue chippers; high school coaches *make* them. The values and concern of the individual coach will affect the character and the commitment of each of his players. He will influence the *class* they reflect in their play. The offense that he develops will provide the opportunities for them to exhibit the full range of their talents. So, Coach Switzer, with all due respect, the high school coach may re-phrase your comment to read: "Good *plays* make good players." And misdirection can do a lot to help.

To that end we hope this book is helpful.

Index